About the author

Margaret Gullan-Whur is a well-known writer on esoteric topics. She lives in Norfolk.

THE FOUR ELEMENTS

The traditional idea of the humours and why they are still relevant

Margaret Gullan-Whur

CENTURY

LONDON   MELBOURNE   AUCKLAND   JOHANNESBURG

A Rider Book published in the Century Paperback series
in 1987 by Century Hutchinson Ltd,
Brookmount House, 62–65 Chandos Place, Covent Garden,
London WC2N 4NW

Century Hutchinson Publishing Group (Australia) Pty Ltd
16–22 Church Street, Hawthorn, Melbourne, Victoria 3122

Century Hutchinson Group (NZ) Ltd
32–34 View Road, PO Box 40–0 86, Glenfield, Auckland 10

Century Hutchinson Group (SA) Pty Ltd
PO Box 337, Bergvlei 2012, South Africa

Set by Inforum Ltd, Portsmouth
Printed and bound in Great Britain by
Richard Clay, The Chaucer Press, Bungay

British Library Cataloguing in Publication Data
Gullan-Whur, Margaret
The four elements.
1. Philosophy of nature   2. Occult sciences
I. Title
113   BD581
ISBN 0–7126–1429–X

Contents

Ut in mundi primordis, ubi tenebræ cujufque cœli cum partibus lucidis, quas viscositas spirituum in illis conclusorum, informationisque avidorum amplexa est, luctabantur in unica eademque massa, in regionem elementarem contracta.

F   Quamvis

Fig. 1   The four elements: the foundation of all things. From Robert Fludd's *Utruisque Cosmi . . . Historia*, 1617, British Library.

Acknowledgements

This is usually the last page to be written. It follows years of reading (when you can get hold of the books), research (if you have the stamina to push your way past extraordinary obstacles) and re-writing. Abandoned typescript drafts and grocery cartons of notes lie around as testament to a long and largely lonely struggle. Frankly, at this stage, writers feel sorry for themselves, which may be why so many acknowledgement pages seem terse, dry or downright ungrateful.

But it is not all slog and, though many high moments are private triumphs, there are others which spring from the help of people to whom the book is not an all-consuming interest. Nearly every one of these pages recalls effort not entirely mine, and perhaps just two examples will make the point. Mrs Hilton of Southery stopped hair dressing to come out in the rain and scrabble under her coal heap for the long-lost standing stone beneath it, and Peter Murray Jones volunteered suggestions on and off for a whole morning in the Students' Room of the British Library. To all those people who brought the *eureka* feeling – thank you.

The generosity of other people has been exceptional. Firstly, I thank the experts into whose fields I wandered, for their tolerance and far-sightedness in allowing me to write my own book in my own way while gently pointing out serious errors. They do not necessarily agree with what I have said, but I want to mention especially Marcus Gregory B. Litt. D. Phil. and a colleague of Jung, Charles Harvey, President of the Astro-logical Association; and Terry Dukes, Doctor of Buddhist Phil-osophy. All have given time and care to stimulating discussion.

Peter MacFarlane and Mim Topliss Green have further helped with astrology and cheirology, and Anelog has explained his unique Natural Psychology. Countless friends and acquaintances of all disciplines have been asked for comment or verification: again, my views are not necessarily theirs and, again, I am very grateful.

The people who read the earlier drafts of this book also helped, through their interest, questioning and critical comment, to make an unfamiliar theme much clearer. I am especially grateful to Diana Lewton Brain, Bill Armitage, Jill Hargreaves and Ann Staveley. (I have read typescripts and I know just how soon one is no longer flattered to be asked!) Rivers Scott, my agent, has been a good friend both to me and the book, as have Neil Walker and David Clayton of Radio Norfolk's 'Airline'. There is nothing like broadcasting for disciplining terminology. And thank you, Bill (Armitage), for turning my cut-and-paste chaos of the elements into a clear word-processed whole.

My family know how important this book is to me, but my husband Jeremy's interest assumed new dimensions when he became official photographer. Biologist daughter Amanda has been a strict inspiration, my mother a continual support, and my son Richard a valued devil's advocate. Perhaps only the families of other writers can know what they have had to endure at times.

M. G-W.
May 1986 Norfolk

Introduction

The whole of this book is an introduction – to a simple and fundamental concept which lends itself equally to immediate intuitive understanding or to prolonged and profound study. Until the seventeenth century, fire, water, earth and air were though to compose between them the whole of man's environment, and everything encountered in life was believed to come within their scope. Although Empedocles, a Greek philosopher of the fifth century before Christ, put forward as a physical theory the notion that these four elements were the basis of all matter, he was but voicing in the West the ancient cosmology of the East, and it is mainly to the East that those wanting to make a deeper study of the subject must turn.

Scientific analyses made since the seventeenth century mean that the four elements are now known as the elements *prescientific*, but it is still generally held to be true that the world began when a spinning mass of fire flew off the sun to form solid material (earth), and that its steamy atmosphere gradually cooled and separated into gases (air) and shallow oceans (water). We must return to this very simple concept of the beginning of our world and its life if we are to get to the root of the four-element idea. It was only through the cooperation of these elements that the first organisms evolved and multiplied and when, in due course, man's hominid ancestors rose to their feet, began to use tools and earned the title of *homo*, they knew that they were totally dependent for their existence on these four vital essences.

Our early forebears are not believed to have thought objectively, but to have felt and sensed the world about them. Not understanding the principles which lay behind the workings of the elements, *homo* imagined the winds and the water, the earth and the sun itself to be inhabited by gods and spirits who, if angered, might play terrible tricks, hurling them about in storms of destructive fury, or withholding their powers altogether. After all, he could never be sure that the sun would rise each day, that the rain would come – or stop, that the trees would continue to bear fruit, or even that the sky would not descend to crush everyone. We smile now at such fears, but only our understanding of scientific principles prevents us from sharing his experience. Try standing silent and alone in the countryside at night, forgetting all learned knowledge of the universe, or watch the behaviour of birds and animals during an eclipse of the sun, as they hide in fear because it seems to be dying, and you may have some sympathy with man's early belief that, because a thing moved or changed, some power must have moved it. Charles Darwin describes his dog barking in terror at a parasol on his lawn as it slowly turned over in the wind,[1] and no one who has had to convince a horse that there is nothing behind a hedge will be in any doubt that the origins of religion arose in part through our animal beliefs in mighty and invisible powers.

Numerous creation legends testify to such ancient superstition. (And let us be sure from the start that superstition is simply outdated religion: the creeds of the twentieth century may one day answer to such a name.) In China, for instance, a colossal divine man called P'an Ku was thought to have given heaven and earth their form. His tears made the Yellow and Yangtze rivers, and when he breathed the wind rose. When he looked round the lightning flashed, and when he died his body fell apart, forming the five holy mountains of China. His eyes became the sun and the moon.

Most settled communities which have left us clues to their life styles tend towards a strong consciousness of supernatural control within the elements. The great temples of Sumer, dedicated to the gods of the sun, air, earth and water, the cave paintings in Africa of rain-supplication rituals, and the *akua* of Hawaii – kind gods of a gentle climate – show us how widespread was *animism*, the belief in invisible beings who dwelt in the elements. In hot countries the sun was a scorching fire-terror to be appeased, but the weak, fitful sunlight of a northern winter had to be coaxed to return, often by rituals using fire. Lesser spirits inhabited trees or rocks, but the great four were to inspire particular awe until at least the end of the Roman Empire. In many places seasonal rituals dedicated to gods of the elements continued long after such deities had officially been replaced, for as long as flood, famine or earthquake still threatened it seemed sensible to play safe. Orthodox religion was dictated by the priestly classes who studied man's past and predicted the future, claiming knowledge of hidden things through their 'hot line' to the gods. No one dared argue with the official arbiters of religion but when, much later, monotheistic creeds forbidding element worship were introduced, playing safe took a very long time to die, lingering on in some rural areas to this day.

As early as 6000 BC *Homo Sapiens* was a literate, skilful and aggressive creature who contemplated his own nature. His body, he knew, was composed of and depended on the four elements: his blood heated by the sun, his chest constantly refilled with air, and the whole kept alive by the passing in and out of water and the fruits of earth. But there arose amongst the thinkers of the East the conviction that the *mind* of man was also conditioned by close contact with the elements, or governed by the same creative force; that the mind was itself a little world, containing the elemental qualities of the greater world, with the same creative and destructive power. They saw a connection between the dynamism and energy of fire and the spontaneous thrusting of the human spirit; between the still or turbulent depths of water and the current of emotional or spiritual understanding which flows in the human breast. They knew that the function of providing food, shelter and fertility was housed in the earth, and that the human mind must include this urge to survive. They noted the refusal of air to be trapped or held down from its high, all-seeing position, and they likened it to the human capacity for seeking out knowledge and passing it on.

These four psychological or internal elements became part of many metaphysical and religious patterns. Hinduism, Buddhism and the Sufi sect of Islam use them in their teachings,[2] the Chinese elements differing slightly; the influential scholars of

ancient Greece argued over their properties, and the psychologist C.G. Jung found them to be an inspiration. For many
people in the West, acquaintance with them is solely through
superficial glimpses of astrology, yet in the Middle Ages, when
ideas filtered into North-West Europe from the Mediterranean,
the balance of the four elements within the individual was of
such universal importance that numbers of new words came
into use. We do not hesitate to describe people as 'earthy',
'fiery', 'gushing' or 'head-in-the-air', but we no longer believe
that character actually results from a physical and psychological combination of the elements. Antony's description of
Brutus in Shakespeare's *Julius Caesar* sums up not only that
belief, but all the ancient - primeval - notions that man is a
product of natural forces and is subject to their four influences:

> His life was gentle, and the elements
> So mix'd in him that Nature might stand up
> And say to all the world, This was a man!

The four element idea deliberately tied human beings to
their physical environment, and this aspect of the concept has
particular relevance to modern living. Of course we meet no
gods or spirits as we fly through cloud banks or descend to the
sea bed, but then neither do we have much respect for the
elements: many of us avoid personal encounters with our
ecosystems as much as possible, encasing ourselves in the streel
shells of our cars or the double glazing of our homes, insulating
ourselves from the smell and the taste of rural air, the feel of the
earth and the sight and sound of water. Human beings are still
an animal species, and the way in which technology-age man
has largely lost his feeling for the natural world makes it
necessary to impress this point. Fringe activities and pressure
groups tend to reflect and compensate for the deficiencies of a
society, and today's dissident prophets deal invariably with our
relationship to nature. They state, in brief, that we are in
danger of destroying ourselves through technology, through
drugs, through pollution and through nuclear weapons. Such a
clear message may often be hysterically expressed, but it
springs from a basic disquiet felt by many. And so we deliberately link each psychological function with its counterpart in

nature, reminding ourselves of the properties of those primordial elements:

Fire: Innovating, leading into action;
Earth: Practical implementing, using the five senses;
Water: Feeling, responding;
Air: Thinking, analysing.

All four elements are equal in status and throughout this book are listed in random order. The ancients realized the importance of their correct balance, too, and the perfect power produced by their blending: the quintessence – *quinta essentia* – the fifth element – represented this perfect blending and was the focus of philosophical and spiritual searching. We shall not be pursuing it in this study for it is a stage which follows complete understanding of the properties of the four elements. It is a good idea, though, to know from the start that all the elements are equally valuable and that, whilst all their truths are valid, none of them can ever be a final authority because each can only be *one quarter* of the truth.

The Greek physician Galen reconstructed the element lore of Pythagoras into a system of types who might be expected to behave in predictable ways. Similar cosmic beliefs lay behind the infinitely more complex patterns of astrology, thought to have originated in Babylon. You may have heard that because of your date of birth you are supposed to be a fire, earth, water or air type, but the synthesis of fourteen celestial influences said to compose the birth chart makes the matter very much more subtle than that. The addition of astrology to Galen's medical system meant that no small amount of learning was necessary for its most elementary application and, although it has now been discarded, its residual truth is that people do function differently. Because different life forces or psychic energies are dominating them, they cannot be expected to see life or to respond to it in the same way. It has been suggested that, ideally, all four elements should function equally; in practice they rarely do, since we are predisposed by heredity, conditioning and environment towards a personal evaluation of thinking, feeling, practical or innovating impulses. When these evaluations form a certain hierarchy or pattern we may be described as a type. None of us thinks we are a type, but we often refer to others as our type!

The ancients believed that if you were strongly influenced by the warmth and movement of sun or fire you were a fiery type, a firebrand; you fired things off and were afire with enthusiasm. Pioneers, leaders and all who would achieve must have plenty of this element in their make-up. (Fire-dominant readers will have read half of this book, probably from the end backwards, before they bother with the introduction.)

If you were chiefly attuned to earth you stayed close to earthy matters, practicalities and the sensible functioning of things. You were never out of touch with reality; you worked hard at down-to-earth projects and, secretly, you found people less earthy than yourself unrealistic and frankly a little daft. (To those earthy, people who are already wondering if they have wasted their money I say this: if this book only suggests one working application which changes your attitude to yourself and others, it will have been a bargain.) The earth type functioned through pragmatism and common sense, and would look sideways at those who seemed to live in the clouds, the head-in-air types whose affinity with air seemed to produce their airy-fairy ideas or a need to air their opinions.

These people, the thinking, intellectual types, lived in a world of abstract reasoning and reflected that element of the universe which pervades all things, vital but unseen, sifting and linking areas of knowledge. (Airy people will appreciate the copious booklist and precise references to factual sources contained in this book, as well as the drawing together of a large number of historical and psychological threads).

People who identified their most natural impulses with the movement of water – and, indeed, they loved to be near that element – were attuned to a mysterious, silent flowing of the feelings which owed its impressions not to reasons but to an instant knowing which engulfed the mind and guided its actions in an almost unconscious awareness of what had to be done. Such types were noticeably impassive towards the practical or earthy side of living; they were slow to initiate action – to fire things off – and they had little to do with the cold reasoning of air which did no more than ripple the surface of their watery depths. From their quiet well of awareness might

gush *expressions* of feeling – art forms or caring gestures, or floods
of suffering tears. Such readers are water witnesses who stand
at the entrance to the unconscious and represent the lost
quality of our century, the ability to respond through feeling
rather than productive thought or action. Whatever they feel
about this book is right for them; it is their truth.

Of course very few of us are so unbalanced that we reflect
only one of these four elements. If we are, we become the readily
recognizable archetypes of dreams or fiction, answering to
nicknames like the over-airy Professor Brainbox or the ultra-
earthy Plain-Jane-and-no-Nonsense. Archetypes are trapped
in their mould, projecting upon the world an image of one sole
facet of its nature. And with that imbalance comes the inevitable weakness of the other elements which remain, archaic and
undeveloped, outside the understanding. Jung drew inspiration from many ancient cultures and concepts, and used their
principles in formulating his psychological types: he recognized
the difficulties which could arise from the lack of attunement to
one 'element'. The first four chapters will tend to reinforce this
point, since the qualities of the elements work unconsciously
within us. If, after reading these four chapters, we decide that
one of them repelled us or was difficult to grasp, we can be sure
that there, across that element, lies a shadow of incomplete
experience and understanding.

No scholar this century has interpreted the four elements
more profoundly than T.S. Eliot, whose *Four Quartets* were the
inspiration for my researches,[3] and no one has put them to
more practical use than C.G. Jung, and yet they remain
strangers to most of us. This book attempts to show that,
whether or not 'much of philosophy has been barren for more
than 2000 years and is likely to remain so'[4], some ancient
wisdom has a great deal to contribute towards the *essential*
balance vital in man's unchanging and unfulfilled destiny.

'Who wants a system on the basis of the four elements, or a
book to refute Paracelsus?' was the 1870s' cry of Dorothea
Casaubon in George Eliot's *Middlemarch*. 'New discoveries are
constantly making new points of view.' This book is not
concerned with systems, and it is certainly not a typology. Its
purpose is to avoid patterns and to concentrate instead on the
ingredients or elements which make each final, unique pattern.

Their cooperation is only possible in the mind and in the wider world if they are separately valued, and whilst this study refers to established syntheses it remains an introduction.

Its symbolism cannot be complete. Civilizations and religions rise up and perish like bubbles on the surface of a stream, and their nature and colouring reflect, during their brief existence, the conditions which surround them. The many examples of ancient elemental imagery which illustrate this book are not conclusive: libraries and museums are full of unexpected tributes to my theme which emphasize its universal nature.

The backward glances of this book graft us to the common roots of our humanity, and help the mind to absorb and retain later ideas. They also show why it is so much harder for Westerners to live in bonded harmony with the material elements of nature than for people of the East whose religions have sustained their contact with the universe instead of striving to subdue it. Their element concepts sprang from a profound contemplation of the nature and possibilities of a mystic yet physically all-encompassing life pattern. Each is a lengthy study in itself and the reference list suggests further reading. But at this point, as we re-encounter humankind's most primitive responses – believed by many to survive genetically intact within us[5] – we must be aware that, before our present civilization, there were others as great, as literate, as complex and as searching.

I

Fire

The only hope, or else despair
Lies in the choice of pyre or pyre –
To be redeemed from fire by fire.
'Little Gidding', *Four Quartets*, T.S. Eliot (Faber and Faber)

The poet Eliot believed that fire, water, earth and air were the elements of man's existence, but also of his dismissal from life. When he wrote that any action was 'a step to the block, to the fire, down the sea's throat or to an illegible stone', he not only clothed his imagery with much of the unconscious fear of the Western world towards its surroundings, but recalled those ancient gods believed to dwell in the elements and to control them.

To early man these gods were true elementals, composed of the material which housed them: of it, yet dominating it, their responses restricted to its natural qualities yet capable of manipulating its force from peaceful cooperation with the other elements to turbulent and mighty destruction. The god was the element: it bore no other name and it obeyed no other god.

During the several thousand years of self-education since elapsed, man has translated those natural forces first into symbols of a natural pattern and, finally – as far as he may – into servants. Yet still they retain a disturbing power, and those who work in direct and daily contact with them acknowledge their implicit authority. Four hundred years ago Spenser depicted earth and water as the mortal enemies of man:

On th'other side an hideous rock is pight
Of mighty magnes stone, whose craggy clift

Depending from on high, dreadful to sight,
Over the waves his rugged arms doth lift,
And threat'neth down to throw his ragged rift
On whoso cometh nigh; yet nigh it draws
All passengers, that none from it can shift:
For while they fly that gulf's devouring jaws,
They on this rock are rent, and sunk in helpless waves.

All that is missing from these lines is the name of the god with rugged arms. All that has changed in man's attitude is that he now accepts that the god he is encountering does not exist. A report in my local paper described the results of a sea-wall flood as the apparent work of a giant hand: wind and water had grasped fifty caravans and flung them against a patch of higher ground, and they looked like crushed match boxes.

Earth, water, air, but what of fire, whose most decisive destruction erases the very image of what has been? It is most greatly feared by animals who recognize, perhaps, that this oldest element – first present in the chaos of pre-creation – is also the newest of the four and the force most nearly within man's capacity to create. The ability to ignite and control fire came to mankind during what he now calls the Pleistocene era. It enabled him to venture far from the tropics and semi-tropics in which he had lived hitherto, but ashy deposits up to seven metres thick found at Choukoutien near Peking suggest that, once lit, the fire must not be allowed to die. Its godly properties of heat, light and flaring, tiger-scaring ferocity might not be granted twice.

Until Peking Man learned to ignite fire around 400,000 years ago, the sole source of this primordial element was the sun. Only in spontaneous, inextinguishable flames or volcanic lava had man seen fire, and he saw it as the weapon of a temperamental sun-force which at times seemed set to consume the world. Because he could live only in those parts of our world where heat and light fell directly from the sky, early man depended willy-nilly on this blinding ogre. Unable to control it, he worshipped it as both morning and evening enlightener and noon-day destroyer. Other elements vital to existence were also to be invoked or conjured, but many cultures are known to have made the sun their chief deity, for without its favour the earth was plunged into icy darkness. If angered, it might glare with

Fig. 2   Sun-Face-Fire Macaw strides across the sky, a flaming torch in either hand. From the Mayan Almanac *for Agriculture, Museum of Mankind.*

scorching ferocity, burning up vital produce and withering human life. (Fig. 2.)

We do not know when man first began to speak and apply names to objects, so we cannot say at what juncture the brilliant and omnipotent orb in the sky became *he* rather than *it*, but the solar nature is invariably recorded as masculine. Crude sun gods, dating back into pre-history, were named after the element itself, and the Greek Helios and his Roman counterpart Sol were part of a line of solar deities scarcely distinguishable despite differing names. Oates records that Marduk, sun god of the Babylonians, completely superceded Enlil, the god of storms, and took over his identity. Apollo, Mithras and Elagabalus might all be worshipped at one shrine, born as they were of one omnipotent force.

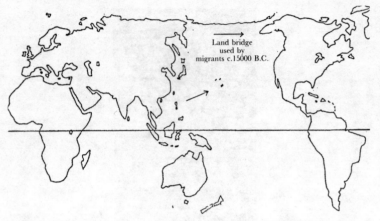

Fig. 3   Eastward movements of population and the isolation of North-West Europe until recent centuries.

Those races who inhabited temperate or northern areas have left us in no doubt of their perception of fire as an offshoot or gift of the sun, and of the ritual significance of both. Tan was a Celtic sun deity and his name meant fire, but in dull and chilly lands where the sun seemed forever on the point of desertion any god introduced from a land which received greater solar blessing would be eagerly invoked. The Roman invasion of Europe added new and powerful sun deities to those worshipped locally, and although animism was by then to some extent overtaken by polytheism – the worship of many gods – the sun's dominating force remained supreme. So truly was its loss dreaded that the Objibwa tribe of North America shot arrows at the eclipsed sun to rekindle it. Northern Europe, westerly limit of the known ancient world (Fig. 3), has left few traces of early structured religious practice and was relatively slow to move from polytheism to monotheism yet, ironically, the East was to see the last official sun-worshipping creed. The Shinto religion of Japan is based on the Sun as Parent, and it was only in 1946 that the Emperor divested himself of that divinity.

Brutal and harsh as were the first sun gods, it is clear that our ancestors distinguished, many thousands of years ago, between the destructive and beneficial aspects of solar power. According to Starzecka, Kane, the Hawaiian deity of sunlight, combined in his kindly creative role the gifts of the other elements and left the fearsome qualities of fire to the raging goddess of volcanoes, Pele. The Chinese Tao (Way) looks at the positive and negative sides of all things; and its early cosmic philosophy symbolized this choice in the dragon which can use its fire-breathing energy for good or ill. Although this concept may have been less consciously grasped by other cultures, many of their gods personified separately the benign and malefic aspects of solar power. Grannos (Irish for sun) and Balder were among those gods who represented the blessings of sunlight in Europe, whilst Tan and Loki inspired dread. Loki, bringer of destructive fire and the Norse god of strife, is said to have plotted the death of Balder whom neither human nor Vanir (spirit of a natural element) would harm. Loki was chained to a rock but legend had it that, at the coming of the Twilight of the Gods, he would break his bonds and unleash a fire which would consume all the other elements, destroying the entire world, its people and its gods. This legend, as we shall see, was echoed in the beliefs of the Celtic Druids. Woden, Norse king of all gods, had for his single eye the sun itself, typifying the lesser role of that great light in near-arctic lands.

Latitude clearly influenced local feelings towards the sun and his works, so it is at first surprising to learn that Shamash or Utu of Sumer, one of the earliest sun deities to be named, was the son of the moon god and protector of the poor. This gentle concept, originating as it did in a hot climate, makes more sense when we realize that, although southern Mesopotamia may now be desert, in the sixth millennium BC the land between the Tigris and the Euphrates was mainly marsh. Thus Shamash was not a scorching tropical terror but an enlightener; in this capacity he is often shown passing judgement. (The ancient civilization of Sumer has left us both its mighty temples and its sun-baked tablets indented with pictographs, neither of which were washed away when the two wide rivers altered course.)

Fire is basically solar energy, but its force was gradually seen as possessing unique qualities, and sun-fire imagery became enriched and extended. In Vedic Hinduism[1] Agni was the first and most awesome of the gods, dwelling in the sun, in lightning, in domestic fire and, later, in the flames of the sacred sacrificial ghee. The cosmic creed of the early Egyptians embodied

Fig. 4 The fire-spitting uraeus, *weapon of the Egyption sun gods and eventually a symbol of kingship. It is still used in witchcraft.*

sun-force in the lion aspect of the sphinx (this is still considered the source of the astrological Leo's vitality and power) but Lurker describes other sun gods representing differing points of the solar day. Re ruled the noon. Fire was symbolized by the eye of Re and was depicted in the *uraeus* (Fig.4), the fire-spitting serpent head which consumed the enemies of the sun gods: the fire goddess Wepes wore it on her head and eventually it became a symbol of kingship. So we see how the growing and deepening of religious belief invests its symbols with more than physical power.

We cannot account for the development of all imagery or for many of the ancient rituals connected with fire. Whilst some rites are well documented, others were secret and the property of the magi, the initiated; yet others remained a living aspect of rural community belief, detached from the evolved practices of priestly sects. Even so, a picture emerges of mankind's acquaintance with the elements and what he came to learn of their patterns of behaviour. Though a wise and experienced man would understand the more refined or mystical qualities of fire, he would also remain aware of the problems connected with its negative, destructive or inappropriate force. The Indian poet Tagore (1861–1941) was attuned to every movement of nature and recognized irreligious use of its power:

> In that emptiness, again,
> have come in bands, along iron-bound roads
> in fire-breathing chariots
> the powerful English,
> scattering their energy.

So, as we come upon profounder and more subtle interpretations of what fire has meant to mankind in the past, let us remember that these are but one aspect of its nature.

In a concept which was to enter many religions, fire was thought to be destructive yet beneficial. In ancient Egypt torches were lit to cleanse the dead from earthly defilement, but the damned were punished in a lake of fire, shown in pictograms by wavy red lines. The adoption of fire as a searing, regenerative force is a long step from crude sun worship; it was brought about through man's continuous awareness of the behaviour of the natural elements. Zen Buddhism calls fire the destroyer of illusions and likens reincarnation to a house on fire – a process of death, sacrifice and rebirth. Though warning that excessive zeal or anger – which Singh says is also a Hindu aspect of fire – burns, Zen Buddhism sees in its flame the direct intuitive arrow of wisdom which enlightens 'in a flash'. As in other religions, a sacred flame burns beside the altar in Tibetan temples, and the Buddhist who speaks of fire without being burned by it is remaining detached in the face of divine enlightenment. The angel of God appeared to the Israelites in flames[2] and spoke from a burning bush,[3] and the Vestal Virgins of Rome guarded the sacred fire which was only allowed in procession with those of imperial, semi-divine rank.[4] In *The Lay of Havelock the Dane* a mysterious flame issuing from the mouth of a sleeping baby convinced its observer of the child's royal birth, for all Scandinavian kings were thought to be descended from the god Woden, and fire was the element of the gods.

The sanctity of religious fire generally depended upon its being freshly kindled and not taken from an existing source. As such it most nearly approached the pure state of heaven-sent fire. This pursuit of complete purity was to occupy both Taoist alchemists and their Western successors. Eliade tells of experimental efforts made some thousands of years ago to recreate the elements by understanding their origins, and that principle will be relevant to later discussions in this book. The *needfire* obtained by friction was supposed to defeat sorcery and cure diseases ascribed to witchcraft, and both men and cattle might be driven through its flames. Bord describes such an Irish celebration of the summer solstice in 1782, and Frazer

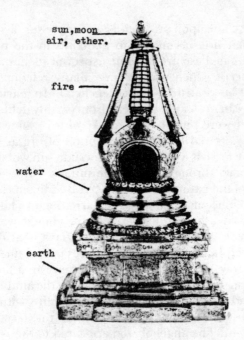

Fig. 5 The stupa forms part of Buddhist element symbolism. Often a shrine or temple, this small gilt model is in the British Museum.

found the practice of chasing needfire across the fields to be widespread throughout Europe.

Many ancient creeds used fire as a symbol of the divine. As the property of the gods – a tangible sun token – it was thought superior to the natural elements of air, water and earth, and was placed at the highest point of the element hierarchy. John the Baptist spoke of the fire which the coming Messiah would use as being superior to baptism by water, and Sufism calls fire the holy spirit, the essence of the divine in man. In the Buddhist symbolism of the *stupa* or shrine, the thirteen steps of enlightenment are placed within the upper spiral which denotes fire (Fig. 5).

The stupa was the basis of all Eastern temples. Originally a sacred monument, it became a shrine after the Buddha asked for his remains to be placed in one. Buddhism recognizes five elements: beyond air, fire, earth and water is ether, the quintessence or integer of the qualities, realms and paradigms described as fire, water, earth and air. Fiery qualities are truth-finding: in Kempo tradition they symbolize the acquiring of skill in all endeavours, the recognition of one's errors and, ultimately, after these truths have been established, the guarding and transmitting of the teachings.[6]

Honoured though fire may have been in these religious syntheses, it was regarded in the West until recent centuries – when vigorous European self-assertion permitted both the recognition of fiery qualities in ourselves and the possibility of trapping their physical terrors for our use – as being chiefly a weapon of the devil. We do not know the exact extent to which the Druids, an elite and priestly caste, dominated Europe, but they wielded power in much the same way as had the Hebrew judges, and their learning, believed to be similar to that of Babylonian, Persian and Greek magi, is believed to have been secret and only acquired after a twenty-year memorizing apprenticeship. Thus it remains clothed in largely unsavoury mystery and it is unlikely that we shall ever know it for certain.[7] But those who claim that the Druids' message was one of cosmic harmony and a better spiritual life after death are not taking into account the profound sense of menace which eventually made the West strive to fetter the physical elements. This struggle is well attested in both artistic and scientific literature, and by the social anthropologist Gellner in the lines which introduce chapter 7 of this book.

The Druids professed to know by occult means the secrets of creation but, in fact, like the Scandinavians, they feared a supernatural and world-destroying conflagration. They are widely believed to have made human sacrifices. Julius Caesar describes the wicker baskets used to pin down their victims before they were burned to death, and Watkins fears that the deep grooves of the strange, east-facing Queen Stone of Symonds Yat (Fig. 6) may have held fast such a cage. Described as a *Tan fana* (Tan – fire, fana – altar), the seven-foot-high stone stands in typical druidic fashion within a circular bend of the river Wye, 'in the face of the sun and in the eye of the light.'[8] This eerie hint of a dark past joins other sombre echoes. Frazer recalls the ritual game – still played in the nineteenth-century Britain – when a chosen 'victim' was swung three times

Fig. 6   The sinister Cwen (Queen) stone of Symonds Yat. It has thirteen grooves, the number sacred to many ancient religions. Photo. J.G-W.

towards a lighted bonfire before being laid on the ground beside it. He might not always have been so lucky. Sometimes an effigy known as the 'witch' or 'hag' was burned on the new year's ritual bonfire. Bord believes it to have represented all the malevolent forces with which the community had had to contend during the preceding year, and that Guy Fawkes on his bonfire is a lingering fusion of that custom with those of Samhain (31 October). But it is unlikely that the human form consumed in the flames was originally an effigy. Frazer quotes the sixteenth-century Spanish monk Sahugan who witnessed the selection and grooming of the Aztec 'scapegoat', a divine victim whose heart was ripped out and held aloft to the sun in ritual slaughter. It seems probable that many cults other than the Druids believed that if the sun were not satisfied with the fuel of human blood in gifts, it would send its servant fire to take earthly life by force. Frazer thought that the sacred trees of the Druids were those most often struck and burned by lightning and, therefore, in need of protective control by ritual.

The Druids also feared the destruction of the world through the bursting of the sea's limits, by the sky falling or the earth giving way, and are believed to have placated the other elements by specifically including drowning, asphyxiation and burial in their sacrificial rituals. We shall see in due course how this destructive religion fed the myth of inhabited elements, and cemented in Western man's unconscious mind the belief that, far from being a shared, living and growing cosmic entity, the natural elements are out to harm us. And the extreme slowness with which this terror has faded under a Christian religion based on love, together with a scientific programme thought by Sagan to be 'increasingly competent to deal with the laws of nature', is acutely relevant to our understanding of our own psychic natures. If we read the accounts of Bede in his *History of the English Church and People,* the records of *The Anglo-Saxon Chronicles* and other early but scanty European literature, we shall find constant anxious references to threatening natural phenomena, for a profound pagan certainty persisted that they were the work of enraged supernatural deities.

The spread of Christianity during the sixth century brought uneasy comfort, for reasons to be discussed more fully later on. Not until the eleventh century would the 'White Christ' reach Scandinavia: elsewhere the Church battled against nature worship, yet Arthur Bryant suggests that its own rituals may have perpetuated fear and the need to placate. Incense had taken the place of burnt offerings, but the intoned or muttered incantation of the *anathema* echoed the Druids' curses and made the fires of hell an almost certain reality. The fires of human sacrifice at death became the inferno after it. The primitive design of intertwining roots found throughout Europe was newly interpreted as an insistence that ultimate death might still lie in conflagration: the text Matthew 3: 10 accompanies the root design in the Black Church – ironically blackened by fire – in Brasov, Romania: 'And now also the axe is laid unto the root of the trees: therefore every tree which bringeth not forth good fruit is hewn down, and cast into the fire.'

All Saints' Eve had eclipsed the sun-fire festival of Samhain, and Christmas had replaced both the winter solstice and the Roman Saturnalia. Legends of the older saints became confused with myths of elemental deities so, when wheels wrapped in straw were trundled across fields in a fiery fertility rite, who could say whether Brigit (Fiery Arrow) or Saint Catherine was being honoured?

It was hard for the bright radiance of the cross to compete with a general concept of fire not far removed from its Gnostic definition of 'the abyss, the abode of the demi-urge and the fount of insatiable passion'; it was also hard to compete with the primordial spinning, consuming mass of world creation. *The Dream of the Rood* (see Sweet's *Anglo-Saxon Reader*) provides a vision of intensely pure white light, the dazzling radiance of God reflected by Christ's cross. But we find its debasement in the fall of Lucifer: light (good) becomes fire (evil):

> 'In the fire lay other fiends, who'd fought against their Lord.
> They suffered torment in hell's midst from hot fierce flames and fire;
> colossal flames and bitter fumes, vapour and darkness, for they had neglected the service of God. Their pride,
> the arrogance of angels, brought them down.
> They would not worship the word of the Ruler of all.[9]

Anglo-Saxon poetry contains central European influences and, within it, we find constant and vivid reference to the positive and negative aspects of light and fire. Celt, Norseman and Teuton alike retained a lively loathing of the devilish gods of fire, and a lingering fear that the forces of holy light would be unable to vanquish them. Though the Celtic bard – a word believed by Williams to come from the Hebrew for 'kindler of fire' – came eventually to inspire fire in the hearts of his listeners rather than upon the sacrificial altar, the maturing philosophies of the East and Middle East were not to influence the Northern races for a further millennium.

It is important to see how isolated was this North-Western end of the known world. The Americas, then absent from world maps, had in any case been reached through the Bering Straits of Alaska or by Pacific crossings from South-East Asia, and their rituals, some of which we shall encounter, show even now curious links with the Middle East. The ancient creeds of Hinduism and Taoism and the complex religious rituals of Egypt were amongst those which developed in great measure from a metaphysical understanding of the physical world. We should do them dishonour if we tried to summarize their element syntheses as these are inseparable from the main body of belief; we can, at most, draw comparisons with events in the

Western world. They differ intrinsically from Christianity in that they sprang from man's nature, rather than – in the way of prophetic creeds – superimposing abstract rules. Whereas Buddhism's origins lay in Hinduism – the Buddha being the ninth incarnation of Vishnu – the Christian faith was the offspring of Judaism, a monotheistic belief in the superiority of man to all other forms of creation, and in his answerability only to the laws of Yahweh. Natural laws, the behaviour patterns of the universe, represented to many cultures a direct expression of the will of their creator and we shall find, during the course of this book, that this option has been generally lost to the West.

Five hundred years before the birth of Christ, the philosophers of ancient Greece debated the importance and functioning of the four elements. To the hypothesis of Empedocles was added the humoral theory of Pythagoras, the system of balance between the body fluids which was to be the basis of European medicine for over 2000 years, and the closest the West was to come to a positive cosmic understanding. Pythagoras's theory echoed Vedic and Oriental belief in its ordering of bodily matter and later, when Galen's system demonstrated additional qualities of behaviour, the fire-dominated person would be known as the *choleric* type, after his predominant choler or yellow bile.

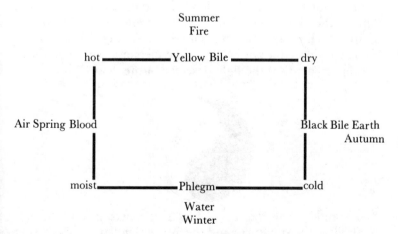

Not until the thirteenth century would the popular teachings of the Greeks reach North-West Europe, and words depicting fire as a human quality come into use. Early medieval texts suggest that the hallmarks of the fiery or choleric type were unpleasant and fearful, certainly far from divine. In our culture fire-raising was still, even if unconsciously, connected with malevolence, and choleric behaviour was thought equally repellant, as we shall later find out. It would be many centuries before fire-brands were considered inspired leaders, and a study of old texts – which we shall look at more closely in chapter 5 – makes plain that the element most admired in Europe was air, a situation which, despite an improvement in the image of the fiery, has not changed.

Yet in the East and Middle East lay a long tradition of respect for the fiery temperament, and to this day fire is thought in many philosophies to be the highest and most enlightened of the elements. The Greek metaphysician Plato believed that an Eternal Being, a creator god who set the world in motion and ordained all living things to be of fire, earth, air and water, used fire in the main when creating the lesser gods, the planets of the firmament. To them was given the task of creating man from the four elements – a loan repayable to the cosmos at death – and the gods used fire to warm the blood and veins. Blood could be raised to near boiling point by passion, but continuous fire produced heat and fever.

The choleric type's hot-blooded nature made him thrust himself ahead for good or ill, and it is the energy and impulsion of fire which remain its first symbolic meaning. In the Tao,[10] fire is considered a powerfully Yang element, whose qualities are represented by the lighter sector of the T'ai Chi symbol:

Fig. 7

Yang stands for all that is light, active, conscious and male: it symbolizes the sun, birth and the future. *Yin* represents all that is dark, passive, unconscious and female: it symbolizes the moon, death and the past. The dark Yin contains a seed of the light Yang, and vice versa, so conflict is avoided and the two suggest harmonious, complementary forces. The poles of dark and light rotate and to Jung, who was to use the symbolism of the T'ai Chi in his study of the human mind, this circular movement had 'the moral significance of activating the light and dark forces of human nature, and together with them all psychological opposites of whatever kind they may be'.[11]

The small Yin seed, present in the Yang and therefore in the fire element, may be taken to symbolize the secondary meaning of fire – the single flame of direct inspirational zeal which bypasses reason and practicality and betokens a vision or an ideal. 'Cloven tongues like as of fire,' indicated the coming of the Holy Spirit (Acts 2), and the Olympic torch is passed on in a single unifying gesture of spiritual ambition. The freedom flame of Berlin is kept perpetually alight, never to be extinguished until the city is reunited. The Buddhist arrow of intuition, and the arrow of Sagittarius which wings towards wisdom beyond the horizon, are a part of the flame symbolism which sees fire not as a force, but as swift and dramatic enlightenment.

Both aspects of fire embody passion, enthusiasm and desire. Paul wrote of sexual burning[12] and we still talk of 'old flames'. It is the heat, vitality and dynamism of fire which distinguish it from the other elements, and this was recognized by the ancients. We do not know whether the Greeks based their theory of humors on Vedic medicine, though Inglis believes so: certainly the Middle-Eastern world appeared to embrace the Yin-Yang concept in its religious beliefs. The Roman sun god Apollo was patron of creative and imaginative learning, but also of prophecy: he looked upwards and to the future. Sun, fire, sky and air tend upwards, whereas earth and water tend downwards and hold the secrets of the past. 'The Great Plan' of the *Shu Ching* states that (the nature of) water is to soak and descend; of fire, to blaze and ascend. This is the active-passive pattern of the elements, felt, sensed or systematized in countless cultures, in the fourfold balance of human nature and in its all-encompassing environment.

Let us look more closely at the way in which the fire force behaves and manifests itself in human nature.

Fire is both heat and light: it radiates, scorches and melts; it shines individually and it enlightens other areas. It is *active*, enthusiastic and self-assertive; it initiates, explores and leads. It gives to, or devours, its fellow elements without blending, though it can be extinguished by them, too. Its nature is to thrust and it will duck and dodge, flare and spark to maintain its own spontaneity.

Psychologically, fire may be used in many ways which correspond precisely to these physical properties. People who function strongly 'in fire' generally appear self-willed. They may act without premeditation or consideration for others and thus, to their own dismay and confusion, have to learn many lessons the hard way. But whilst it may scorch others, over-functioning in fire also damages the fiery individual himself, who is inclined to use up all his resources and burn himself out both mentally and physically. No one can function in one element alone, and fire tends to harness another element and use it passionately, exhausting the mind and the body.

Fire, used in the inventively intuitive sense of a truth-seeking device, registers mental ideas and is embodied in Jung's *intuitive* psychological type. This 'innervating' intuition (Jung's word) picks up notions and activates them, an attitude deeply distrusted by strongly earthy individuals, though they, too, have the propensity within them to develop it. This kind of intuition (the word simply means the bypassing of reason)[13] has nothing to do with feelings. The nature of this kind of sensitivity is that of radio antennae, and the following extract from Thomas Carew's 'Elegie upon the Death of the Deane of St Paul's, Dr John Donne' illustrates it to perfection:

> But the flame
> Of thy brave Soule, (that shot such heat and light,
> As burnt our earth, and made our darkness bright,
> Committed holy Rapes upon our will,
> Did through the eye the melting heart distill;
> And the deepe knowledge of darke truths so teach,
> As sense might judge, what phansie could not reach;)
> Must be desir'd for ever. So the fire,
> That fills with spirit and heat the Delphique quire,
> Which kindled first by thy Promethean breath,
> Glow'd here a while, lies quench't now in thy death.

(The Delphique quire uttered divine wisdom: Prometheus stole the gift of fire from Olympus.)

Those who function weakly in fire lack enterprise or drive. Fire is needed to innovate or initiate, to 'get a thing off the ground', and wasted talent is almost always due to poor fire functioning. In assessing the handwriting of proven 'achievers', Gullan-Whur found that the uniting factor was a refusal to be deflected from a chosen course, an apparently necessary degree of obsession. This is a fire quality, and one not easy to bring into conscious function at will. Books on positive thinking aim to deflect the downward and inward impulsion, and to inflame drive and desire upward and onward towards future goals. The smallest understanding of the nature of fire tells us that the most likely way for this to happen is through the fanning of an already-present spark: but it is also vital to fix a future goal, to be a visionary with an ultimate state of achievement ever in view. Once this pillar of fire exists in the reality of the mind, all unconscious impulses will move towards it, accepting only those alternatives which further its attainment and discarding those which decoy.

Functioning in balance, fire warms and enlightens the world. Genius, spirited talent, 'intrudes and disturbs',[14] but such intrusion may be negative, evil genius if used to burn. Any consideration of this element should take into account not only the difficulty of igniting it, but also the problem of quenching its life and fuel-seeking intensity. Playing with fire is thought folly even within such a fire-orientated civilization as that of Western Europe. Modern technology is a strong fire force, and may be creative or destructive according to its application. Early man awaited the consumption of the world by fire, and if the over-use of technology (fire using air, dominating water and earth) continues to escalate, man may achieve this all by himself. Solar energy is produced by nuclear fission in the sun. Its use by man on earth in nuclear reactors could certainly lead to the total destruction of life on this planet.

By itself, fire does not obey reasons (an air function), consider practical results (earth), or respond to the promptings of feeling (water). It follows hunches, moving forward and upward in the pursuit of its own dynamic desire. To have purposeful function it must be linked to another element, and without

such harmonious partnership it can represent insanity, a total
lack of balance.

2

Water

I do not know much about gods; but I think that the river
Is a strong brown god – sullen, untamed and intractable,
Patient to some degree, at first recognised as a frontier;
Useful, trustworthy, as a conveyor of commerce;
Then only a problem confronting the builder of bridges.
The problem once solved, the brown god is almost forgotten
By the dwellers in cities – ever, however, implacable,
Keeping his seasons and rages, destroyer, reminder
Of what men choose to forget. Unhonoured, unpropitiated
By worshippers of the machine, but waiting, watching and
waiting.
'The Dry Salvages', *Four Quartets*, T.S. Eliot (Faber and Faber)

Water is traditionally thought to be the natural and irreconcilable enemy of fire, its qualities in all respects anitpathetic. The Channel Islanders of Victor Hugo's *The Toilers of the Sea* recoiled from the 'devil boat' powered by steam, and their preacher questioned 'whether man had the right to make fire and water work together when God has divided them'. The alcohol of white man's 'fire-water' inspired the same awe as did the strange and fiery phosphorescence of fish; both, like the flame-red spots of the salmon, indicated to many of their observers the certain presence of the supernatural – the manifestation of the impossible before their eyes. Shakespeare's Bolingbroke voiced medieval disquiet about the combination:

Methinks King Richard and myself should meet
With no less terror than the elements
Of fire and water, when their thundering shock
At meeting, tears the cloudy cheeks of heaven.

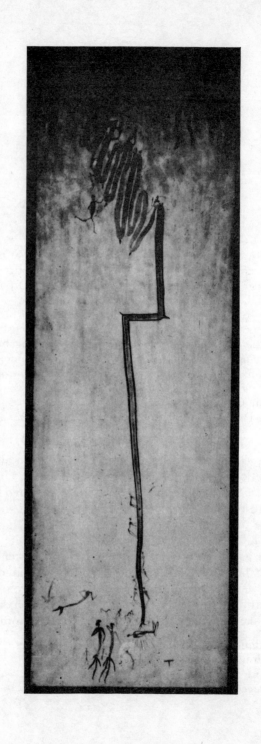

Be he the fire, I'll be the yielding water:
The rage be his, while on the earth I rain
My waters; on the earth, and not on him.[1]

But Aquinas, in his study of the nature of essence, was convinced of the reconcilable properties of all the four elements, and in his *Summa Contra Gentiles* states that even fire and water can cooperate in their behaviour to form a system. We shall find, during the latter part of this book, that this combination is not only capable of harmonious productivity, but constitutes a well-known behaviour pattern of the human environment.

Nevertheless, if we are to immerse ourselves for a little while in the cool and unhurried reaches of the water element we must be prepared, like Tom in Kingsley's *The Water Babies*, to slip away from action and striving, doing, conquering and achieving, and drift downwards to a different world. It will not be, as Tom discovered, without its own surges of discomfort, but their movement will be of a new nature and texture, of a lapping diffuseness of rhythm unencountered in the brightly lit buzz of fire-flair.

Eliot recognized the particular power of water – the godness enclosed within its liquid form – and hinted in 'The Dry Salvages' of a retributionary strength which might take the unwary or disrespectful by surprise. This idea goes back to biblical and druidic dread. In fact, water only responds in the way it must, a concept which applies equally to all four elements and on which understanding the meaning of this book depends.

It might be supposed that ancient water religions were concerned only with the survival of men, animals and crops, and indeed benevolent spirits were thought to refresh man and his world with gifts of rain. But these gods did not represent the profoundly mystic qualities of water which had other, more subtle rulers.

The fertility aspect of this element plays less part in early symbolism than the powers connected with water masses, deep or flowing water. In lands where most water fell from the sky,

Fig. 8   The African Rain Tree. East African Wahnge myths explain that, in this rock painting, a virgin of the royal house is buried alive beneath a tree, causing the rain goddess to send her gifts. Photo. Queen Victoria Museum, Harare, Zimbabwe.

Fig. 9   The Mayan turtle Bacab. Sky gods sent the rain, but the Bacabs seem to have been blamed if the crops failed. Drawing from a stone carving, Museum of Mankind.

rain had to be induced (Fig. 8) and the Hawaiian fertility god Lono and the Mayan deity Imix were amongst those who gave or withheld this vital sustenance. But where water sprang up from the bowels of the earth or gathered into pools, lakes and oceans there, universally, dwelt mystery and wisdom. Water, of all the elements, was by nature the most arcane.

Gods who inhabited springs and river sources were attributed with primeval, all-knowing power. The Egyptians believed that the Nile spring was made to gush by the hermaphrodite Hapi who, in ape form, dwelt within the cavern at its fount. Thompson suggests that, to the Maya, the ultimate power over water lay with the turtle or tortoise who could live beneath it without drowning, yet could abandon it and live beyond man's span of life without a drop. The turtle represented one of the incarnations of Vishnu, the Hindu god who later visited earth as Krishna and the Buddha; it was also believed to have wise and mystical qualities by many American Indians. (Fig. 9). Fenimore Cooper relates in *The Last of the Mohicans* how it was venerated and thought at one time to have carried the world on its back.

In Europe, trees were thought to have an affinity with water, and to draw up its wisdom through their roots. Offerings were made through them to water spirits to ensure that nearby springs and wells did not run dry, for even in a wet climate standing pools could become foul and quickly kill a whole community. (To this day, pieces of cloth are tied to hazel branches beside the Madron Well in Cornwall.) But the wisdom drawn up in the sap, and found by the Druids in the berries of the mistletoe, closely resembles the sacred milk of Vedic India – later to sanctify the cow itself – and may be connected to religious rituals little understood by those who simply asked for water to feed the body.

The Roman god Neptune, a fresh-water deity before he merged his identity with the Greek Poseidon, was worshipped on 23 July each year to avoid a midsummer drought. He, too, came to signify mysticism and hidden wisdom, qualities traditionally conferred in astrology by the planet which was named after him.

Water gods and spirits were generally, but not always, the friends of mankind. The Sumerian Enki or Ea is shown by Oates in one tablet with fish pouring from his shoulders. Half goat, half fish, he is thought to be synonymous with Oannes, the primeval man-fish of the Gnostic faith; he also features in Indian Vedic texts. Obscurely, this hybrid figure was an early symbol for the astrological *earth* sign of Capricorn.

Enki was the holder of secret wisdom which he might be persuaded to pour out with his fish. But the symbolism of water generally suggests that to learn its secrets you must go down into its depths and submerge yourself, like the Egyptian god Osiris who had to be drowned before learning the truth about death and regeneration. The Camenae, Roman goddesses of a sacred spring, held the gift of prophecy but, as wishing wells still dictate, many gifts had to be thrown in before an answer came. Excalibur, the sword of wisdom, was lifted from beneath the waters and in Norse mythology the Norns, 'knowers' of past, present and future, guarded the springs at the roots of Yggdrasil, the sacred ash tree.

In many cultures the unfathomable depths of the ocean, believed in ancient times to surround the world, were thought to have housed and given birth to primeval man. 'Water babies' are a remnant of this myth. The hermaphrodite Hapi of the Nile held the secrets of sexual origin but Nun, the Egyptian god of primeval water, was credited with generating all things. (Fig. 10) The warm womb-bath from which the human baby emerges at the moment of birth may lie behind this mythical understanding and mankind's need to return from time to time

Fig. 10   Nun, the god of primordial water, lifts up the morning sun-god Khepri. In ancient Egyptian creation legends Khepri (often shown as a beetle) begat Shu the air god, father of Geb and Nut.

to this safe and dreaming world is another story, to be introduced later in this chapter and discussed thereafter.

Poseidon was the Greek deity who ruled the ocean, could cause earthquakes and, like the mysteriously named Davy Jones,[2] chose and guarded the drowned. Equally mysterious but yet more terrifying were the water-monsters who lurked in lakes and pools; we may no longer fear the mighty Grendel[3] in this country, but we are still none too happy about his descendant in Loch Ness! The Anglo-Saxon word *thurs* indicated a place of evil water where monsters were thought to dwell. The Celtic races also believed in spirits of river, spring and pool, many of which survive by name if not in ritual. Westwood describes amongst them the old woman with long green fangs known as Jenny (Jinny) Greenteeth, still thought in 1908 to lurk below stagnant, weed-covered water in the hope of catching unwary children.[4] Like the Russian Rusalkas with their green teeth and green hair, Jenny Greenteeth seemed to personify the weedy and ensnaring aspect of such water, and

Westwood suggests that this myth was in part kept alive by mothers who wanted their children to stay away from deep water. This does not explain the many sources of sacred water, inhabited by gods and goddesses of benign charity, in which a child, or for that matter an adult, might easily drown.

To the Celts, evil water was ddu (black), whereas sacred wells and springs healed and their water was called wen (white). Both founts were propitiated with symbolic gifts (which may at one time have taken the form of live sacrifice) and the Romans were known to show respect for the local deities. Conventina's well, near Carrawburgh, was found to countain coins and offerings dating from pre-Roman times to the fourth century AD. The Druids believed that serpents guarded sacred wells; several snakes are sculpted on an undated and disused font in Kilpeck church, Hertfordshire. Sul was the Celtic guardian of healing waters and those at Bath were named Sulis Minerva not only to honour her but also in Roman homage to the goddess of wisdom.

Water which healed seems to have been an accepted phenomenon worldwide: put another way, one of the properties of the water element was traditionally considered to involve the physical removal of disease. Miraculous cures by immersion – which continue today within the structured practices of spa bathing – were not always due to occurrences contrary to the known laws of nature (as the term miracle would imply) but to happenings within the human body unanswerable to reason. Though few Western doctors accept the healing value of mineral-laden water – despite its orthodox use in Eastern Europe and other countries – they are united in trusting plain-water immersion to relieve many types of pain.

Most ancient cultures included medical treatment within the scope of their religion. Imhotep, chief architect to King Zoser of the third Egyptian Dynasty (c.2900 BC) was also renowned as a physician. In time he became a kind of demi-god, patron of the learned and all who would master the secret arts. He was finally accepted as the god of medicine and, according to Gregory, those who sought to write wisely would pour out a few drops from their water jar as a libation to him before dipping in their pens. Jesus used saliva in several acts of healing – though that pagan practice was forbidden under Jewish law – and founded the Christian mission of ministering to the sick. This book is at times severely critical of those who have distorted the teachings of Christ in the centuries since his death, but all credit must be given to the work of the Church in bringing compassionate comfort to that suffering sector previously believed to be harbouring devils of illness. Inglis tells us that the first hospitals were founded by Christians.

We shall return to this mainly watery concept later, but we are still concerned at this point with the behaviour of the water element itself and with the qualities traditionally associated with it. We have seen that its magical properties were acknowledged throughout the ancient world and that its unconscious wisdom was thought to be imparted to those who could attune themselves to its arcane rhythm. So deeply were most cultures soaked in this belief that the new Church of Rome had no choice but to authorize 'holy' water of its own consecration and to make judicious use of the many sources of water which were already venerated before they were christened holy (*halig* – hale or whole). By the time of the Kent mission in AD 597 a policy for handling pagan sites had been perfected, and Abbot Mellitus was told to adapt rather than destroy the existing arae or fana (heathen altars).[5] He was to see that they were asperged with holy water and so converted to altarae, Christian centres of worship. Later, churches were said to have been built near wells to ensure a supply of water for baptism, yet a three-year fast was imposed in the seventh century on those who offered sacrifices to fountains, and this ecclesiastical denunciation was repeated in the laws of Canute and by Archbishop Anselm in the eleventh century.[6]

The asperging of sacred sites was of course a form of baptism (Greek for washing), and we shall soon come to appreciate the significance of such cleansing as a mental process. The Ganges river purifies the soul as well as the body and, as in many other religions, Sufism regards the spiritual cleansing of baptism as the first development of a higher consciousness. Palmer tells how Chang Tao-ling, a Taoist astronomer and alchemist of around the time of Christ, encouraged spiritual healing through water-purging. The individual would write out all the sins and failings of his life and then, embracing his written confession, would wade out and immerse himself in a river.

Water qualities are not limited to the mystical or supernatural, and the element is capable of powerful, at times overwhelming, response. The destructive properties of fire were so often manifested to early man that they featured vividly in his cosmic beliefs. But all the natural elements have the propensity for violent and unbalanced activity and, though water may have been used by the gods to help man, it could also be employed to annihilate him. The waters of the Red Sea were said to have been parted for the Israelites to permit them to live,[7] but the God of the Jews inflicted hail and rivers of blood on their captors,[8] and the ultimate in punishment – the Flood – upon his own people when they corrupted the earth.[9] The myth of the flood exists in many cultures, and torrential rain was a terrifying threat. Druidic fear that the sea might burst its limits led to human sacrifice by drowning – a deliberate and devastating suggestion that the elements would snatch lives recklessly if not bribed first. Bord quotes the ritual sacrifice of a goat by Scottish fishermen before putting to sea, and their more symbolic placing of a white stone on a certain cairn recalls the pebble gifts of Pacific Islanders. (Fig. 11)

The moon was known to have a special relationship with water long before its influence on tides was proved. (Its place in early religion demands a separate study). Lunar phases were also known to control menstruation,[10] and the Hawaiian goddess Hina was one deity believed to have governed this moon-water force. Since the human body is now said to be 90 per cent water, who is to say what other interactions may be discovered? As we have seen, the ancient Greeks attributed all disease (lack of bodily ease) to disturbance in the equilibrium of the *humors*, a word which means moisture. Although by a direct psycho-physical link it was the origin of our modern *humour*, I am going to keep to the Latin spelling throughout this book as a reminder that, until the sixteenth century, all humors were fluids. To Plato these fluids or *phlegma*, 'sweat and tears and similar liquids daily excreted', could, if excessive, cause boils or affect the brain, and we shall find before long that the *phlegmatic* character may well be prone to the ills of suppression or damming-up.

As with fire symbolism, the Tao and Buddhism provide the earliest definitions of the mental qualities of the water-ruled.

Fig. 11   Wood and feather figure of a sea spirit, from the Solomon Islands. Museum of Mankind. In Pacific Island cultures the sea-gods' goodwill was sought by adding a pebble to the sacred pile on the shore.

To the Chinese, water is depth of feeling, its negative quality being ineffectuality – 'wetness'. Zen or Ch'an Buddhism sees it as the profound response of the unconscious mind, capable of dissolving the earthbound 'ox of clay'. This religious school scorns the usual doctrinal apparatus of scriptual rules and depends totally on enlightenment through meditation or direct inspirational revelation: Zen Buddhism strives to pass beyond the intellect; to know rather than to learn. Jung speaks of the value of the Eastern way of life which permits a consciousness which does not create itself but 'wells up from unknown depths'.

The records or legends of early civilizations show the waters of life and death in symbols of fertility or drowning. But the second symbolic meaning of water in the ancient world was profound mystical wisdom only to be acquired by humans through an unconscious response. The three water signs of astrology embody between them all these concepts, with Pisces, the last of the twelve, receiving the soul into its depths.

To the ancients water was the source of all life. The spring was the mother of the stream, and the stream was the mother of the lake. Though the process of giving birth may appear active and creative it is a Yin, passive process, the carrying-out of the will of a Yang creator-spirit. The psychological qualities of water are therefore 'receiving' ones, and can only be put to active use by fire or air.

The gods and spirits of water either guarded the secrets of life in submerged realms, or they offered them to those who could use them. Abraham decreed that Isaac should take as his wife the unknown woman who offered water,[11] and it was water, symbol of wordless compassion and understanding, which was shared by Christ and the woman of Samaria.[12] It is because water has always – in Western alchemy (Fig. 12) as well as the Eastern Tao – been thought of as passive and feminine, that a woman is often depicted as its bearer. Traditional painted jugs were sometimes made in the shape of a woman's torso, the spout placed between her breasts. (I found two such jugs in the Brukenthal Museum, Sibiu, Romania.)

The shades of feeling embraced in a compassionate gesture of outpouring could scarcely be more eloquently expressed than in Tagore's poem:

Fig. 12   *The four elements of alchemy, from the* Quinta Essentia *of 1574. Air and fire were traditionally male forces; earth and water female. The surrounding zodiac signs are in circle order, not element groupings. Britsh Library.*

The battle is over. After strife and
    struggles the treasure is gathered
    and stored.
Come now, woman, with your golden jar
    of beauty. Wash away all dust and
    dirt, fill up all cracks and flaws, make
    the heap shapely and sound.
Come, beautiful woman, with the golden
    jar on your head.

The play is over. I have come to the
    village and have set up my hearth
    stone.

Now come, woman, carrying your vessel
    of sacred water; with tranquil smile
    and devout love, make my home
    pure.
Come, noble woman, with your vessel of
    sacred water.

The morning is over. The sun is fiercely
    burning. The wandering stranger
    is seeking shelter.
Come, blissful woman, with your full
    pitcher of sweetness.

The day is over. The time has come to
    take leave
Come, O woman, with your vessel full of
    tears. Let your sad eyes shed
    tender glow on the farewell path
    and the touch of thy trembling hand
    make the parting hour full.
Come, sad woman, with your vessel of
    tears.

The night is dark; the house is desolate
    and the bed empty, only the lamp
    for the last rites is burning.
Come, woman, bring your brimming jar
    of remembrance. Open the door of
    the secret chamber with your
    unbraided streaming hair and
    spotless white robe, replenish the
    lamp of worship.

> Come, suffering woman, bring your
>   brimming jar of remembrance.

Rabindranath Tagore,
Collected Poems, Macmillan

The most commonly used symbol for water is a vessel, showing that it needs to be contained. Aquarius the water-carrier, eleventh sign of the zodiac and, according to *Oedipus Aegyptiacus*, the direct descendant of the Egyptian god Canopus, is a man, a masculine air symbol who actively pours out the waters of wisdom contained in his jar for the benefit of mankind. The complex combination of air and water – at first encounter a contradiction in terms – can only be assessed when the nature of the air element is fully understood. And we have yet more to learn of water.

By itself this element is formless but, once channelled, it assumes great power by flowing, falling, eroding or submerging and, in so doing, its responses are unconscious. It may be boiled, turned to ice, sprayed, evaporated or allowed to form lakes; thus it is unstable yet indestructible. It is inert and cannot prevent itself from being moved, nor can it move without help from the other elements. Quite often it remains underground, to rise suddenly under pressure.

Fresh water may have been worshipped and desired during the entire human occupation of Western Europe, but its symbolic properties have seldom been welcome there. As either emotion or spirituality they disturb, so are popularly restricted to the reflective expressions of ready-produced art or such caring human responses as nursing. (Even here water must be linked with another element for, by itself, it merely feels, responding to events which touch it with wordless compassion or revulsion.) Reflected expression does not require us to make a downward journey to unexplored depths of feeling or to unconscious experience, the 'dark interior soul-life only fitfully illuminated by dreams', of which Jung accused the whole Western world of being afraid.

Certainly the West has tended to preoccupy itself with two aspects of water only: the negative feelings enshrined in the words 'wet', 'gushing', 'drippy' and 'soppy', which suggest that all expression of emotion is better absent, and the strongly positive qualities of tangible art forms. We shall soon be meeting the miserable medieval figure of the water-ruled *phlegmatic*, whose public image was to plummet still lower with the onset of the cultural movement of the seventeenth century, attributed to Descartes and known as the age of reason. That movement, which elevated the intellectual processes of the mind to a status which reduced the body and all its impulses to a 'thing', is properly discussed in relation to the air element, but is mentioned now because the water-consciousness it so derided was eventually to gush forth in the defiant and jubilant cascades of the Romantic rebellion.

The neo-classicist restraints of the eighteenth century, about which we shall hear more, caused distress and fury to those who preferred intuitive truth to reason and, in sympathy with the French uprising against social and cultural shibboleths, they roused themselves to make a stand on behalf of the senses. In growing numbers and across most of Europe, the Romantics of the late eighteenth and early nineteenth centuries vehemently denounced reason, claiming that the real truths about mankind could only be reached through unconscious, feeling processes; that the noblest human qualities lay in profound awareness rather than intellectual productivity; that the divine element was not air but water. Blake went so far as to identify intellectual pressure with the temptation of Eden: 'serpent Reasoning . . . Two-Horn'd Reasoning, Cloven Fiction'. The Romantics tried to arouse passion and mysticism, to reawaken in man that which defied analysis and to restore his sense of harmony with – rather than domination of – the world of nature. Perhaps Wordsworth, whose watery flow was no turbulent torrent but a deep and tranquil spiritual response, best voiced in 'Tintern Abbey' the dim cravings of the West for a happy relationship with the cosmos:

> For I have felt . . . a sense sublime
> Of something far more deeply interfused,
> Whose dwelling is the light of setting suns,
> And the round ocean and the living air
> And the blue sky, and in the mind of man;
> A motion and a spirit, that impels
> All thinking things, all objects of all thought,
> And rolls through all things.

This *knowing* of a truth which could never be proved through science or instilled through instruction, and the possibility of encountering a divinity through that awareness, suggests that spirituality is an unconscious function, neither man-made nor truly to be experienced through his doctrines. Modern religious sects which activate unconscious and irrational responses are generally distrusted in Europe and America. Discussion of the air element will explain why such fear is partially justified, yet it remains true that spiritual awareness is a water quality. (Note the rosary held by the phlegmatic character in Fig. 25). Plato reminds us that this kind of intuition is a low-based receptivity rather than a fiery mental inspiration: it is for him, literally, a gut reaction:

> And knowing that it would not understand reason or be capable of paying attention to rational argument even if it became aware of it . . . god played upon this weakness and formed the liver . . . making the part of the soul that lives in the region of the liver cheerful and gentle, and able to spend the night quietly in divination and dreams, as reason and understanding are beyond it . . . and gave it power of prophecy so that it might have some apprehension of truth.[13]

Water-sensitives – mystics – have lived in all ages, but the Western attitude of recent centuries has made it hard for them to share their vision. The dualists' split between the mind and the senses began to place an artificial value on consciously rational and productive behaviour: activity and alertness impressed, but stillness and silence, the downward and backward directing of earth and water, became unfashionable to the point of abhorrence. (Dr Johnson is recorded as saying that he hated a 'Feeler'!)[14] To this day in Europe it is not considered normal simply to sit doing nothing, and anyone entering a room and finding someone sitting awake but with closed eyes is likely to think they are ill. The practice is quite rightly associated now with transcendental meditation, a passive technique relatively recently introduced from the East, where enlightenment is thought to come from downward and inward searching.

Here in the West we have always been taught to 'Lift up your hearts, and lift them to the skies.'[15] This need for a lifting of the mind and spirit away from the senses has resulted in a barrier between the outer and the inner life, one whose painful effect is most clearly to be seen in nineteenth-century attitudes. Because behaviour was so frequently unrelated to feelings but whipped into set shape through superimposed self-restriction (later to be revealed by Freud as the workings of the Super-Ego), moral stances were often staged. Inward looking was regarded as unhealthy and, although Altick notes that a feeling came more easily to them than a reflection, the 'Victorians' were forced to repress a great deal of psychic energy because so little of it was socially acceptable. The intensity of the Romantics had dwindled into sentimentality – a peculiar misunderstanding of the water function – and practical morality. Kingsley's *The Water Babies* offered a poignant allegory of a dream world, but in *Ambervalia* (1849) Clough pin-pointed precisely the problem of his age:

> How often sit I, poring o'er
> My strange distorted youth
> Seeking in vain, in all my store
> One feeling based on truth; . . .
> Excitements come, and act and speech
> Flow freely forth; – but no
> Nor they nor aught beside can reach
> The buried world below.

The Anti-Victorians Carlyle, Dickens, Arnold and Morris had their counterparts throughout Europe, but the Pre-Raphaelite movement in art reflected rather than compensated for the unsatisfactory inner life of the period. The 'watery response' was not generally understood or appreciated amidst the fire-earth prosperity of the industrial revolution or the airy rationality of positivism:[16] a cartoon of 1880 shows an 'aesthetic' gentleman seating himself in a pastrycook's and ordering a glass of water, in which he places a single lily to gaze upon!

Although some nineteenth-century hymns showed a groping for profound religious experience, their implicit comment that respectability and prosperity were 'not enough' in no way approached the spurning of gain and comfort that were to typify the over-watery flower-power cult of the Western post-war world. Though charismatic spiritual movements have released the water function in part, the West suffers still from undervaluing of the feeling response.

Emotion, as the word suggests, is moved or disturbed feeling (water) and is a particularly unpleasant aspect of this element to the predominantly air-earth British ideal. This is not true of the so-called national temperaments of other European nations, and certainly not of the American ethos which encourages the exteriorization of feeling. That long and clumsy word is well worth getting the tongue round and savouring: it means exactly what it says and the very understanding of it is a first step towards preventing watery blockages. Though the British stiff upper lip presents a commonly recognized caricature of the problem, people of all races do suffer from the problem of unexpressed emotion. In his book *The Origins of Love and Hate*, Suttie entitled one of his chapters 'The Taboo on Tenderness'. He believed that, whilst women are permitted to react emotionally, the ways in which masculine affection are disguised in horse-play, group-joining and jokingly derogatory remarks means that men are artificially differentiated from them. Forbidden to weep from an early age, many men lose touch with their emotions and, when women are brought up to conceal their feelings, they cannot help others to release them. The feeling function is ideally one quarter of the whole, and only requires one quarter of our attention but, when this is denied, we experience repression.

Such poor functioning in water bears an interesting resemblance to its physical counterpart. Water washes, removing unpleasantness which otherwise might cause trouble, and, if the washing process is not fulfilled, if the water does not flow naturally, congestion occurs. Damning up this flow causes physical illness and mental distress, and the greater the natural propensity for watery (feeling) response, the more serious this is likely to be.

Emotional problems occupy a good deal of doctors', psychiatrists' and the clergy's time, and are very painful for the sufferer and those around him. Many theories for coping with stress and unhappiness which seem to have no natural outlet or solution have been put forward, and Jung and Freud used dreams to search for the hidden stumbling-block. Attitudes buried deep in the unconscious may not gush forth easily, but the steady flow of everyday feelings may prevent them from going underground in the first place. Again the direct relationship with water itself is interesting. We have discussed the inexplicable benefits of watery immersion in relieving pain and even curing disease, and we have touched on the security enjoyed during our nine months of floating in womb water. There may be a link. Many diseases are now thought to have their origins in repressed feeling, and physicians such as Pearce find evidence for this claim in past instance and present research. Lying or, better still, floating in warm water may put the senses back in touch with what they need and miss, and may encourage the flow of unconscious response. Showers merely wash; they do not allow the body to be one with the water. Water-time, in a pool or in the bath, can be used as a conscious invitation to the feelings to make themselves known, and it goes without saying that crying in the bath is supremely therapeutic. Those who, like Clough, are aware of a deeply buried world which they cannot reach, might attain water through water.

Many people function strongly and habitually in water, however, and know exactly how they feel at any given time. They rate their emotional or spiritual sensitivity highly, considering it a truer guide to decision making than any other of their faculties, and find no cause to explain themselves or their actions in rational terms. 'That is how I feel about it,' is, for them, ultimate wisdom. Calmly flowing water (feeling) influences without dominating but, unless it is channelled, it may become a torrent which hurtles uncontrollably, swamping the other three elements and totally engulfing the self.

Far beneath the profound and tranquil depths of the untroubled feeling faculty lies the spiritual aspect of water. It is latent in every human soul, but such purification cannot be reached unless the turbulent or dammed-up waters of emotional response spend their passion and lie still, in released and total calm.

3
Air

Other echoes
Inhabit the garden. Shall we follow?
Quick, said the bird, find them, find them,
Round the corner. Through the first gate,
Into our first world, shall we follow
The deception of the thrush?
'Burnt Norton', *Four Quartets,* T.S. Eliot (Faber and Faber)

The symbolism of air in human history relates to its invisibility and the loftiness of its inclination. We shall see later how, for centuries, modern man has placed his faith in its abstract qualities, in contrast to the chilly terror this unseen sky-borne force inspired in his forebears.

On the whole, air and sky gods of the ancient world were cold, hard and often hostile to mankind. They hurled down hurricanes and whirlwinds upon the earth, enveloping in this displeasure threats of worse to come. *The Anglo-Saxon Chronicles* show that, as late as the twelfth century, they were considered omens in this country and, to this day, hurricanes are given names. Only occasionally did air deities look kindly downwards: the Mayan Ecatl carried gifts of rain in his breath, and the Egyptian Shu (Fig. 19) was the benign supporter of heaven – the intangible source of all outer, *super*-natural knowledge.

The concept of heaven arose, we believe, from the cloudy notion that the means of creating or destroying life came primarily from above. The earth which bore crops could not do its work unless rain came, and the thunderbolts and lightning – later considered the property of fire – seemed warnings that at any moment the whole programme could be switched off and the world deprived of the essences it needed for survival. The Sumerian sky god Anu was lofty and superior in character and thought to be the ancestor of royalty, but he was eventually replaced as king of all deities by his son Enlil, the god of storms. Possibly it was recognized that the sky did not send the fire which made lightning so terrifying, and that fire was the property of another, more powerful god. Mackenzie tells us that Gaelic charms recall the storm god as 'King of the Elements'.

Whatever it sent, 'heaven' wielded power of an active, *Yang* nature. Because the sky was considered the route to heaven, rainbows were seen as a mystic bridge across it and, in the Mithraic religion (based on sun-worship), the sky was visualized as a tube of air hanging down from the sun. Cooper believes that the descent of Father Christmas down chimneys is a folk memory of this.

The belief in a great heavenly force above the sky could also have stemmed from an *all-seeing* concept since, from that position, nothing on earth could pass unnoticed. Consequently, creatures who could rise in air currents to this position were thought to act as messengers and, in a similar fashion, winged messengers from heaven were able to float to earth and appear as angels. Birds occupied a special position in the religions of many cultures, and the respect paid to a hawk or eagle has older and deeper origins than admiration for its keenness of eye.

The eagle will be found time and again to represent the powers of air, powers which embody not only knowledge gained through outside aid but also the ability to communicate, discriminate and thus be cleverer than one's neighbours. At no time was this more important to our ancestors than in battle: the bird of prey could hover and observe what was going on amidst the enemy – an ancient concept fully borne out by modern aerial warfare. We shall find that air knowledge was all too often linked with the need for supernatural aid in battle: the early Christian Church swiftly adapted this tradition by making the eagle into the peaceful bearer of divine airy instruction, as seen in the emblem of St. John and on bible lecterns.

Airy knowledge in battle was a remarkably widespread concept. The Egyptian sky god Horus was represented by a falcon's head, and the later war-victory god Montu wore a

Fig. 13   The Cretan griffin supports the judgement of King Minos, Knossos. 2000 BC. Photo. J.G-W.

two-feathered falcon's head to lift him above the vulture, thought to give protection in battle. Bird heads and feathered heads signified status and power through air knowledge in Hawaii, and were symbolized by the mighty, totally feathered war-god Ku whose effigy is to be seen in the Museum of Mankind (London). The Aztecs and Red Indians are noted for their ornate bird dress, and the multi-animal symbolism of the Middle-East (Fig. 13) is reflected in Fenimore Cooper's Mohican warrior who '. . . painted three faces for himself – one in front, while on one side he appeared like the beak of an eagle, a litle open, the eye and the head perfect, and on the opposite side the same nose represented a hog's snout, with a small eye, and showing the teeth very skilfully done.'

The mythical thunderbirds of the North American tribes who lived by the Great Lakes symbolized the forces of the Upper World. (Fig. 14) They represented clouds, rain, fertility and life and, as air deities, used lightning against the dark forces of the Underworld. The American Indians gave supernatural meanings to the four winds and believed that, when the body died, the soul rose up through a specially prepared hole, to depart in a spiral of air. The Romans would free an eagle

Fig. 14   The thunderbirds of the Great Lake tribes believed to be the friends of man and to use lightning to fight evil. (See Longfellow's well-authenticated Hiawatha.*) Basket design. Museum of Mankind.*

above the funeral pyres of great men, believing that the spirit thus made its way to heaven.[1]

Jupiter was the Roman god of sky enlightenment and his emblem was an eagle. A statue in Brindisi shows him with an eagle at his feet; it gazes up at him in aweful acknowledgement of his ruler-ship. Jupiter gave protection in battle but threw thunderbolts when angered; in Tibet Llamo and her bird-headed goddesses were of similar character.

So intense was the belief in the eagle's knowledge and external aid that the following legend may be true. It is said that the barbarous Nahua tribe, seeking a site for their capital (Mexico City), saw an eagle of great size on a cactus plant, grasping in its talons a huge serpent.[2] The symbolic meaning of the serpent varies from culture to culture, but this image would certainly spell success for the eagle controlled in its victory fertility forces, evil, or supernatural power. Strangely, thousands of miles away in Egypt, King Djiet used this imagery for his insignia. (Fig. 15)

The plumed serpent of the Aztecs was the intermediary of the sun god and represented the powers of wind, rain, thunder and

lightning, making a link with the Lucifer of the Gnostics to whom Satan was the Prince of Air. In Gnostic teachings air was itself 'the consolidation of earth's grief'. Snake images are confusing and diverse and it is perhaps best simply to remember the supreme, airy power of the eagle. Yet devils, too, had wings – Satan was but a fallen angel – and the Venerable Bede describes a battle beneath the heavens between good and evil forces of knowledge. It took place amid blood-red skies and tempestuous winds, portents of the anger of God towards man.

Centuries after Western civilization developed its own languages and literature, the most powerful of all gods was still thought to dwell in heaven above the sky, and to wrestle with evil knowledge in the air. *The Anglo-Saxon Chronicle* records what is now believed to have been the *aurora borealis:*

> On the Tuesday after Palm Sunday, 22nd March (AD 1121), there was a very violent wind; after which numerous portents appeared far and wide in England, and many heresies were seen and heard. . . . In the same year, on October 20th . . . there were many sailors on sea and on water who said they had seen a great and extensive fire . . . which continuously increased in width as it mounted to the sky. And the heavens opened into four parts and fought against it as if determined to put it out, and the fire stopped rising upwards.

But when undisturbed, the skies remained clear and the transmission of superior knowledge was carried downwards to the minds which could accept its intelligence. Being invisible, clear air invariably symbolized clarity of thought. Air was knowledge of a factual and reasoned kind, based on logical comparisons and observation. The Roman Mercury, winged messenger of the gods, had a sharp, subtle intellect and was the patron of merchants and thieves, a concept which emphasizes the idea of air as 'outside' information. But in most religions air or *pneuma* is related to divinely imparted knowledge or teaching, and Plato called speech the 'servant of intelligence' (divine reason). He warned that an excess of air caused breathing dysfunctions and tension, and we shall see that the airy individual is probably more likely, through this tension, to suppress

Fig. 15   Stele from the tomb of King Djiet c.3000 BC. Cliche des Musées Nationaux, Paris.

the flow of his watery feelings than any other type. The *sanguine humor* came to signify a love of the abstract and rapid thought processes which needed constant stimulation.

Zen Buddhists, in their search for unconscious *wisdom* rather than consciously learned *knowledge*, were wary of the harsh and intransigent properties of air and thought that the mind was as illusory and wandering as the wind, liable to be caught up in a whirlwind of excessive prejudice. Singh, a Hindu, noting the qualities attributed to the four elements or *prakrti* of Vedic belief, equates air with greed, an active concept with clear reference to the modern thirst for factual information.

We have heard how Descartes (1596–1650) drew a rigid distinction between the conscious mind (which he equated with a divine soul) and those functions shared by man with the animals. He believed that pure intellect, if properly used, could not fail to distinguish between truth and falsehood, whereas the senses, imagination and emotions might deceive. Descartes, being himself dominated by the air function, was compelled by his own nature to analyse and rationalize each of life's processes. Earlier philosophers had assumed a similar separation of the psyche from the material universe,[3] but Descartes asserted his distinction on the grounds of scientific certainty; his exaltation of directed thought above those mental functions obscured or even caused by the senses was the beginning of an attempt by one part of the human mind (air) to understand the whole. L.L. Whyte notes that only after Descartes do we find the term *unconscious mind* entering European thought, as other philosophers sought to prove that the bodily sensations, emotions and imaginings of human existence were not gross sense perception but valid and equal functions of that same mind which handled intellectual concepts.

So thoroughly did Descartes and his successors implant a doubting attitude – 'to doubt everything which we find to contain even the smallest suspicion of uncertainty . . . what is doubtful should even be considered as false . . .' – that almost all aspects of contemporary European life were challenged. The quoting of ancient authorities ended: the wisdom of the past was tested and many earlier beliefs were quickly labelled as superstition. The satirical scholar and poet Alexander Pope, equally cynical towards men of science or imagination, saw the dilemma into which dualism had thrust modern thinkers and, half a century after Descartes, voiced the doubts of many in his *Essay on Man.*

> Know then thyself, presume not God to scan
> The proper study of Mankind is man . . ..
> He hangs between; in double to act, or rest,
> In doubt to deem himself a God, or Beast;
> In doubt his Mind or Body to prefer;
> Born but to die, and reas'ning but to err;
> Go, wondrous creature! . . . Mount where Science guides,
> Go, measure earth, weigh air, and state the tides;
> Instruct the Planets in what orbs to run,
> Correct old Time, and regulate the sun;
> Go, soar with Plato to th'empyreal sphere,
> To the first good, first perfect, and first fair;
> Or tread the mazy round his followers trod,
> And quitting sense call imitating God;
> As Eastern priests in giddy circles run,
> And turn their heads to imitate the sun.
> Go, teach Eternal Wisdom how to rule –
> Then drop into thyself and be a fool!

The sense of disorientation and loss experienced by those whose Yin nature could not easily adapt to the chilly and over-ruling effects of air was widespread in writings of the seventeenth and eighteenth centuries, and was eloquently expressed through the water-consciousness of poetry. Soon after Descartes's *Discours de la Méthode* was published in 1637, Chapman cried out against the 'stepdame Night of minde', who

> Broods beneath her hell obscuring wings
> Worlds of confusion, where, the soule defamed,
> The body had been better never framed . . .
> When earth, the ayre, and sea, in fyre remained,
> When fire, the sea, and earth, the ayre contained,
> When ayre, the earth, and fire, the sea enclosde
> When sea, fire, ayre, in earth were indisposde,
> Nothing, as now, remainde so out of kind . . .
> Chaos had soule without a body then,
> Now bodies live without the soules of men.

The intense inner vision of the blind poet Milton (1608–74)

saw only cosmic order, the hand of God dispensing and controlling Reason. Heaven's Light had been slow to reach the 'dark illimitable ocean' beyond the gates of Hell

> . . . where eldest Night
> And Chaos, ancestors of Nature, hold
> Eternal Anarchy, amidst the noise
> Of endless wars, and by confusion stand.
> For Hot, Cold, Moist, and Dry, four champions fierce,
> Strive here for mastery, and to battle bring
> Their embryon atoms.

When it did:

> Swift to their several quarters hasted then
> The cumbrous elements – Earth, Flood, Air, Fire.

The response of the Churches of State and Rome to the new evaluation by reason was to exert authority through their own dogma. Military, commercial and colonial expansion had put into power men who could argue and persuade, and neither Catholic nor Protestant persuasions were short of learned and clever theologians. What all Christian sects most wanted to dispel was the implicit suggestion that Christianity, too, was a superstition of the past. Whilst for the past four or five centuries the Catholic Church had attacked heresy through the fire-earth force of the Inquisition, it now needed desperately to prove its validity through abstract argument. A scorched-earth approach gave way to the hot-air and windbag politics of synod and soap-box, and the rationalizing, classifying spirit of the age eventually found identity in John Wesley's Methodism (1797). The Church of England was aided by such thinking poets as Milton and Bunyan; the Catholic Church strengthened its obedience to the Vatican and resisted all attempts to make it an instrument of the State. A dissident group, the Quakers, foreswore all rules and ecclesiastical structure, however, and though its societies were established during the 1650s and 1660s it belongs by nature to the Romantic movement.

Western dependence on the intellect gradually increased. Even when psychology, the specialized study of the mind, came into being, and the nineteenth-century psychologist Fechner likened the human mind to an iceberg of which only the uppermost and visible conscious tip housed reason, behaviour tended to be accounted for by scientific experiment closely linked to biological facts.

The capacity for intellectual analysis separates man from other animals and is a vital function of his mind when correctly applied. The point at issue here is that, during the past three centuries, a critical attitude has looked for order in those areas which least concern it – in art, in drama, in relationships between people and their environment, and in religion. The pursuit of reason meant that all over Europe cultural images of classical restraint began to replace those born of the boisterous vigour of the Middle Ages: Kitson believes that the Neo-Classic style in European art 'was perhaps the only movement in the history of art to have been brought into being by critics, philosophers and connoisseurs rather than artists'. We have seen how the floodgates of spiritual and creative energy burst open to demand freedom of expression – freedom from the need for self-explanation – in the Romantic revolution, but we must return briefly to the destructive and usurping role of the intellect in matters of religious faith because it has been, in part, responsible for a damaging lack of harmony in our Western culture.

In Islamic Sufism air is the third stage of enlightenment and governs the teaching or doctrine which follows baptism; and the apostle Paul talks of his longing to 'meet the Lord in the air' (pneuma).[4] Yet air is not the prime element of the world's great religious prophets, most of whom functioned chiefly through fiery intuition and turned to simple, earthy pursuits in order that their spiritual vision might not be entangled by intellectual dogma. Jesus the Nazarene, founder of the West's main structured religion, lived in total harmony with nature. Allegedly born amongst animals, at peace in a tempest, finding spiritual truth in the wilderness and finally dying in a thunderstorm, he consistently reconciled man with his whole nature, filling his teachings with allusions to farming and fishing, winds, clouds, fire, storms, water and sunlight. He gathered children about him and sensually appreciated the soothing gift of the earthy and emotional Mary Magdalene.

Why did nothing of Christ's cosmic unity reach through his teachings to those in the West who so badly needed it? One reason is that cosmic philosophies were part of a pagan past to be shunned – the Gnostic and Essene Gospels are still unacknowledged by orthodox Christianity – and another, that he was badly served by Paul. This apostle of the Gentiles consistently preached against the joy and beauty of the material world, and cemented theology (discussion of God) and doctrine as the cornerstones of the Christian Church. Whereas Christ taught communion with God by the sea and on the mountain, Paul used synagogues, and his mission lies at the core of the bringing of Christianity indoors and into the head. Denigration of the human condition, like the gathering in dark, man-built churches on days when intensely glorious natural beauty seems to sing the creators' praise by itself, is the legacy of Paul and the theologians, but not of Christ. Removal of the Acts and the Epistles from the New Testament reveals a very different religion; one which might have led the West to a more harmonious interaction with the natural world.

The 'Communions' of the Essene Gospels, found amongst the Dead Sea Scrolls in 1947, suggest that Jesus recognized divinity in the elements which surround us. These beautiful verses, of which only one can be included here, tell of direct communion with the angels of fire, water, earth and air:

'And he [Jesus] lifted his face to the rising sun, and the radiance of its rays filled his eyes as he spoke: "The first Communion is with the Angel of Sun. . . ." '

All the 'Communions' show profound empathy with the physical world and the four elements which sustain it, and make humbling reading today: how they would have comforted our Western ancestors. Instead of Paul's injunctions to despise the flesh they would have heard:

> The Lord sent the Angel of Earth
> To make the plants grow,
> And to make fertile the womb of woman,
> That the earth may never be without
> The laughter of children.
> Let us worship the Lord in her.

The man whose trust in the elements allowed him to walk on water did not learn to do so from a rulebook.

As we progress through this study we shall find that a greater understanding of the four elements helps us to relate to the four diverse and apparently conflicting attitudes in our minds. It is then easy to spot those occasions – as in the situation above – when one element seeks wrongly to dominate. The nature of air is to define, regulate and explain – a vital function but only one quarter of our truth, and one whose limitations have yet to be accepted in our present civilization.

We have discussed air a good deal, and discussion is its business! We shall find that the concept of air as knowledge learned *from without* balances and complements the wisdom gained through *inner* unconscious processes: each is valuable and the two need be neither opposed nor confused. According to our concept air is analytical, critical and objective; it observes, makes connections and classifies. It feels nothing, and its properties begin and end in its changeable nature. Static air is not the same as bubbles or dust, a whirlwind or a steady force 4, and although bubbles and dust have admixtures of other elements, air is also variable in itself. For this reason, any attributes given to it are liable to sudden changes. By itself, air has an intangible nature and always needs references and relationships. It is used invisibly in burning and breathing and, in its psychological perspective, it has also to be harnessed to be useful. The body-controlling cults of Taoist alchemy and Hindu Yoga had, in common, breathing rituals designed to bring man's vital need of air into subjection through the will. Their motives were different but their aim was to reach such complete comprehension of the breathing process that it no longer dominated the human frame.

The nature of air is to be disembodied and fragmentary, and this may be the consistent state of the uninformed and illogical mind. The currents of air which shape thoughts into coherent streams are not always regular or controlled: they may be lethargic and weak, leaving 'sails flapping' listlessly, or they may function spasmodically, threatening at times to overturn the boat of the mind through their reckless force.

Air does not represent creative thought in the sense of original or innovative ideas; that is the property of fire. It connects ideas, and thus satisfies curiosity; it finds causes by using facts, and gives reasons by the same method. It makes syntheses, patterns of thought, arranging them without originating them, testing, comparing and proving all new theories. Air deals in abstract systems of reason and criticism at the expense of feeling, practical concern or innovation and, without the help of another element, it has the dry sterility of computerized knowledge. Whilst inventive thought requires the inspiration of fire, practical thought needs an admixture of earth, and the combination of water with air can produce a sensitive objectivity, invaluable in counselling.

People who function strongly in air tend to be detached, informed and analytical. Air is not intelligence, but may be a powerful agent in expressing it. An overbalancing of air creates an intensely critical, analytical mental faculty and, of course, this is constructive if appropriate. It is inappropriate to make mental analyses during moments of physical enjoyment, during a graveside ceremony or whilst initiating action, but very airy people do so, and at times their dithering, their 'ifs', 'buts' and 'maybes' can effectively prevent any action taking place at all! The absent-minded scholar is functioning predominantly in air, although he can develop his other functions if he wishes. When linking patterns of thought he is 'in his element'.

Poor functioning in air results in difficulty in detaching oneself from subjective actions, feelings, needs and wishes. Because thoughts are not easily systematized, reactions may be inarticulate, rash, emotional or heedlessly physical. Bursting into tears or lashing out with the fists is not the appropriate response to unacceptable ideas or an unintelligible mathematical problem, but lack of air produces *unreasoning* attitudes. At times of panic, when archaic reactions threaten to blot out the critical faculty, air must be called upon and put firmly in control.

A closely reasoned mentality means that the air type may have difficulty in comprehending the emotional, spontaneous or urgently physical needs of others, and for this reason intellectual decisions are often considered inhumane. The airy individual may struggle to analyse problems such as violence or (to him) unnecessary emotional involvement. He will weigh and balance causes and relevant data without success until one day he thumps his fist down in exasperation – and understands, through one of his other, neglected elements of comprehension.

What if the foot, ordained the dust to tread,
Or to hand, to toil, aspired to be the head?
What if the head, the eye, or ear repined
To serve mere engines to the ruling mind?
Just as absurd for any part to claim
To be another, in this general frame . . ..

Pope's warning here that reason does not know every answer is a central argument in his *Essay on Man*. But Pope was himself an intellectual and, despite his assertion that 'Tis hers [reasons's] to rectify, not overthrow,' he cannot truly be thought to have had the wholistic vision of Shakespeare. His pretentious claim to be writing a *noble work* on man's place in the universe illustrates the particular ability of the air type to provoke a sullen and, at times, fearful awe. Strong functioning in any element may arouse resentment in other people and, because air's activity takes place inside the close workshop of the head, a powerful air faculty tends to exclude others who may resent being unable to penetrate what they see as secret or cunning thought processes. (This is not invariably true for, although air which is not exteriorized busies itself with the quiet categorizing of facts, extroverted air can be highly political, airing its opinions with considerable force – huffing and puffing, as our culture puts it, hot air!) Even the static, observing aspect of air can be disquieting to those in whom it functions minimally, since abstract brain-work sometimes irritates those who react to life chiefly through the senses.

A total failure in understanding abstract principles can turn this resentment into open hostility. Hooliganism, anarchy and blind charismatic loyalty make an enemy of the air function, pitting against its ordering powers the destructively negative aspects of the other elements. Whilst the Romantic movement was based on a desire for creative expression, the 'mindless' elements – and note the derogatory implications of that word in our culture – so employed, seek only to pull down and destroy the important quarter-part played by the airy, reasoning function. Such negative aspects, recognized thousands of years ago by the Chinese, are not to be confused with the rightful struggle towards equilibrium (caused by the attempt of one element to usurp the role of another) of those who only wish to redress a lack of balance. Those who rebel against all authority, all rules, are not of the same mentality as those who would prefer a more wholistic approach to human truth than has been fashionable during the past 300 years.

The introduction of the word 'scientific' in 1637 prefaced the arrival in our language of many new and limiting terms: Potter tells us that 'formula', 'curriculum' and 'ultimatum' were amongst those which entered our language during the seventeenth and eighteenth centuries. Their potency today suggests that knowledge which has been tested and proved still dominates our culture, making air the most generally trusted of the elements.

The relatively recent growth of interest in magic, self-awareness, natural medicines of uncertain effect and ancient esoteric wisdom may herald the end of Western Europe's long tyrany by air. If it does, man must be careful that he does not create an equally harmful lack of balance of a different kind. The Western ability to maintain order and to find honour in negotiation and compromise is regarded with bewildered envy by those races whose culture does not express it; it is a positive airy attribute. That we have lessons to learn from the East does not imply that it has nothing to learn from us. In mimicking our technological and bureaucratic progress, nations as close as the Eastern European bloc have sadly allowed the masculine elements to predominate dangerously, and we know that over-balancing in any element will tend to bring out its negative qualities.

Air is necessary. We should not want all things reduced to attestable fact but, without the cold, clear wind of informed understanding, our minds would become a steaming tropical jungle, filled with passionate feeling and fertile physical energy, but without order.

4
Earth

Lifting heavy feet in clumsy shoes,
Earth feet, loam feet, lifted in country mirth
Mirth of those long since under earth
Nourishing the corn. Keeping time,
Keeping the rhythm in their dancing
As in their living in the living seasons
The time of the seasons and the constellations
The time of milking and the time of harvest
The time of the coupling of man and woman
And that of beasts. Feet rising and falling.
Eating and drinking.
    'East Coker', *Four Quartets*, T.S. Eliot (Faber and Faber)

Earth, the material from which we borrow our mortal flesh and to which our bodies return at death, represents those matters of practical existence unanswerable to logic or feeling, and slow in plans or progress. In the still dark night there is no sun, no light, no moving air and, at times of drought, no water. The earth remains. Those other planets on which no form of life is supposed to exist are substantial proof that earth is the solid base on which the other three elements function; this was recognized by Buddhism which depicted earth as a cube at the base of the stupa. Plato also assigned the cube to earth, 'for it is the most immobile of the four bodies and the most retentive of shape'.

Small wonder that the earth element was often symbolized in stone. But the forces it stood for in numerous ancient cults were complex, embracing as they did both birth and death and all that man in animal form must suffer in between. It might be thought that stone would be chiselled only into aspects of endurance and, indeed, the Egyptians sought to preserve their dead in obelisks, cementing the individual soul into a concrete object which could not be corrupted by decay. But the Israelites were permitted only unhewn 'unpolluted' rock for their altars as an alternative to the bare earth table ordained by Yahweh,[1] so that they might not make them into graven images. Only the sacred Commandants of the Lord were allowed to be transfixed into stone, giving them the deathlessness of that unmoving substance.

Though stone might be marked by man or used by him to symbolize his concepts, in the oldest of religious origins the stone itself was god. Peculiarly of the world, as opposed to the unseen deities of sky and sun, it nevertheless might seem to have been sent from heaven, for the stone most held in awe was alien, meteorite rock. Sacred stones, those named and set apart as the subject of legend and ritual, are invariably distinguished by their composition, siting or shape. They were power to be feared, yet the powers within them could perhaps be passed to man.

In Europe sacred stones abound. From megaliths to markstones no more than a foot or two high, these rocks may have been connected with earth rites or the worship of sun and moon.[2] Some may have been erected through almost incredible feats of human effort, and firmly anchored down within the soil, while other natural monuments are said by succeeding generations to have been flung or dropped into their grotesque positions by the devil. Because man understood – even before he learned to make marks upon it – that stone was the most durable of all commonly found earthy materials, he made it a focus of his beliefs. In some cultures standing stones were thought to represent dead ancestors and to house traces of their vitality, but twentieth-century researchers are interested in more tangible earth energies. Whether or not stones can transmit the sexual fertility so often claimed in folklore, it is now of academic concern that the energy charge emitted by them should be measured. Despite many scientific experiments the properties of these alleged natural forces are not fully understood, but it seems that 'charged' stones often contain quartz deposits which may attract energy from outside.

Explanations for the placing and meaning of charged standing stones vary: Fidler believes they project negative, harmful energy and were set up to act as warnings. Markstones are stubby and acted as signposts to the alignment of more important sites but, like the larger standing stones and megaliths of Stonehenge, Callanish and other sites they are generally made of rock quite unlike any local stone.

I found such a standing stone at Southery in Norfolk, buried under a coal heap. Within living memory it was considered a potent fertility force: men drank dew from its four-feet high top, and girls perched knickerless upon it at midnight, watched, I was told, by the local gentry who may have contributed to the stone's reputation for success! After my visit a psychic 'sensitive' stood on it with bare feet and was apparently almost hurled off by a powerful emanation of energy – an electric sensation varying from tingling to a strong shock.

Often a charged stone stands up against a church – correctly, the church was placed against the stone – attracting the energies of a sacred site or subduing its evil. Fig. 16) We have already heard how stone altars which may have witnessed human sacrifice were retained, asperged and used in Christian worship, the Church literally building on and around an ancient hallowed rock. It would continue to build and its soaring stone spires – a source of wonder to historians – pointed out the glory of God's heaven above. They were also, according to Bord, a deliberate attempt at pulling sky energies down to earth. This prehistoric image of the marriage of Sky Father and Earth Mother, the cosmic balancing of Yang and Yin, was central to many religions, and the female nature of the earth element will soon become clear.

Ley lines, the perfect alignment of important pagan sites which may be of soil, water or stone, are a study in themselves and are related to the Chinese wind-water *feng-shui*, the art or science of divining the natural forces at work in any piece of untouched land. Practitioners of such geomancy believe that to disregard the inner balance of physical matter by building in the wrong place, is to court adverse – negative – powers. The ancient figure of the *dodman* with his two staves, treading the countryside as he placed one before the other in a dead straight line, is depicted in the hill-cut figure of the Long Man of

Fig. 16   Earth Mother as foundation stone at Braunston Church, Leicestershire.

Wilmington, Sussex. (Watkins reminds us that the word dod-man meant garden snail.) The earth itself was believed to house energy, to be attracted or avoided through heaps of stones or earth, spiral designs or mazes, and those significant yet mysterious standing stones. Tests of this earthy energy – at present so little understood that it has no exact scientific name – show that it may pulse from site to site – along, perhaps, the invisible lines or leys about which there is still a great deal to discover.

The work carried out by Watkins and his intrigued successors – Michel, Graves and Fidler in particular – may have been better understood by early man himself who experienced, rather than experimented with, earth's natural magnetism. Infinitely more sensually aware than modern man, and employing physical functions now dulled through lack of use, he may have perceived the pulses of energy around him and responded to them with animal keenness. When their potency appeared to slow or cease he would try to arouse it for himself, beating the ground through dancing or thumping or – in many cultures including our own – performing the sexual act upon the soil to regenerate it. *The Times* of 6 May 1986 reported the gathering of twenty-two troops of Morris dancers at Headcorn, Kent, in a fervent re-enactment of the Jack-in-the-Green ritual. The 'Jack' is, from prehistoric days, a man disguised as a bush, who dances through the streets – possibly along the track of a now-forgotten ley line – and is finally 'killed' to release the spirit of summer. There is little doubt that the killing was originally far from symbolic, but the fear that summer's vital fertility will never burst forth seems to be undiminished.

Man's capacity for sympathetic attunement to the forces of nature remains intact, and may be highly developed in those with psychokinetic gifts. Such people, who are apparently able to harness earth's energies and deploy them at will, moving material objects and changing their physical form, are less numerous than those who simply live in touch with the elements and come to understand their ways. We shall find that this involves removing, for at least part of the day, the interference which man has put between himself and the cosmos.

The life-forces which early man implored and which his twentieth-century descendants believe they can compel through technology were concerned with the survival of the species – with fertility. Though earth is in itself sterile, its impregnation by a Yang force makes it fecund and fruitful, the provider of all mankind's bodily needs. The phallic shape of standing stones, and the lustful images later carved in stone, reminded and encouraged nature to do her stuff. Material less durable than stone was often used, but stone, some sculpted long after the coming of Christian teachings, endures to tell the tale most potently. Earth's energy is put into her: she does not herself create it: the 'stone dead' qualities of rock imply passiveness and quietude, a waiting and unresisting fortitude to be imprinted with the will of male action and dictate.

> Struck with the curse in mid-wave of
>   your tumultuous passion, your life
>   stilled into a stone, clean, cool and
>   impassive.

You took your sacred bath of dust,
    plunging deep into the primitive
    peace of earth.

You lay down in the dumb immense
    where faded days drop, like dead
    flowers with seeds, to sprout again
    into new dawns.

You felt the thrill of the sun's kiss with
    the roots of grass and trees that are
    like infant's fingers clasping at
    mother's breast.

In the night, when the tired children of
    dust came back to the dust, their
    rhythmic breath touched you with
    the large and placid motherliness
    of the earth.

Tagore's understanding of earth's role depicts a woman, one whose nature is so much a part of our culture, our conditioning and perhaps our longing, that we know her name without being told. Earth Mother always was. The Hindu Prithivi – her name simply meant 'broad' – was one of the oldest of all known goddesses, and the Chinese Queen or Mother of Earth was surely loved for many thousands of years before she was written about in the ancient texts of the Tao. One sign stood for both 'earth' and 'mother' in the truth-divining philosophy of the *I Ching*, and of all the tangible element symbols left to us today the almost worldwide cult of earth-woman, earth goddess, provides the oldest and most endearing.

The land itself bears witness to her indwelling presence. Undulating hillsides, breast-shaped mountains and earthy cave-wombs were both her monument and her body, and there she was worshipped with special reverence. Gifts of small stones were left on hill-tops to form nipple-like cairns: flowers were laid upon her sacred sites and milk poured into hollow stones and gulleys as a libation and a guard against barrenness. Farmers would climb to the very top of the sacred mountain of Abergavenny in order to sprinkle a handful of its soil upon their fields after sowing.[3] The bounty of the earth goddess was seen far above in the Milky Way, christened 'Hera's Milk' by the

Greeks. If she chose, she could pass on her regenerating power to human women, and Bord tells how closely mothers pressed their bodies to the soil during childbirth or revealed their naked, infertile genitals to her in secret ritual visits.

As early as 4000 BC the 'broad' fecundity of Earth Mother was caricatured in lumps or pillars of rock, to be set up and honoured or beseeched. And as late as medieval times her special gifts were still being carved into stone, often – in a religious devotion of mingled origin – on the walls of churches. Fig. 17 shows a Sheela-na-gig, named after a Celtic earth goddess, whose exposed and displayed pudenda immortalize in the most lasting of earthy materials the mortal flesh of woman and her means of procreation.

But the earliest stone replicas of Earth Mother were less explicit. These vast-rumped and big-breasted idols, sometimes pregnant in appearance and at times shaped into portable, doll-like figurines (Fig. 18) symbolized she who gives birth and provides. She was both virgin and fertility goddess, ancient as the stone from which she was crudely hacked, and young as the green shoots of spring when she was traditionally worshipped. She reigned in most parts of the world, earthy Yin consort to sky-fire male omnipotence, dowdy and chaste yet of ravenous sexual appetite. As the Babylonian Ishtar, and Isis, mother-figure of the Egyptians, she was thought to have given birth to both gods and kings, and her sacred gifts of conception and growth were implored with sacrifice.

Ugly and hag-like as she might be depicted, Earth Mother was not only revered, but loved:

'You ask me to plough the ground? Shall I take a knife and tear my mother's bosom? Then when I die she will not take me to her bosom to rest. You ask me to dig for stone? Shall I dig under her skin for bones? Then when I die I cannot enter her body to be born again.[4]

This American Indian's cry seems to have echoed around the world, not only amongst agrarian cultures where earth mother was goddess of vegetation and fertility, but also in hunting communities. Many Siberian tribes believed in a 'mother' who gave life to wild creatures, and afterwards sought to protect them.[5] The earth goddess has always been held in special esteem in Europe. Archeological finds point to her importance

Fig. 17   Sheela-na-gig, symbol of female fruitfulness. Kilpeck Church, Herefordshire. (From Celtic Inheritance, *Peter Beresford Ellis, by permission of Muller)*

Fig. 18   Chalk earth goddess from Grimes Graves, Norfolk. c.4000 BC. *British Museum.*

in pre-history, and in the seventh century BC the founders of the Greek city states dedicated their first temple to Hera, the bronze age Earth Mother later reputed to be wife and sister to Zeus. Tripp points out that the earth goddess was less impor-tant to nomadic races, and it is interesting to notice the increasing favour in which she was held when the Balkan Greeks ceased wandering and created their city states. In her Roman guise of Tellus or Ceres, the Greek gooddess Gaia was introduced to Northern Europe, to merge with Nerthus (the Earth Mother of seven mid-European tribes), Freya of the Scandinavians, the Celtic Brigid, and Eostre the April goddess. 'The mother of the gods' was honoured in a Roman festival of AD 187,[6] but by then her identity might be arbitrary.

Her significance, however, was universal, and is still not entirely dead. The coming of Christianity converted fertility-feast days into saints' days, and prayers in grottoes to earth mothers were redirected to the Holy Virgin mother; but the straw dollies made to honour Brigid (Bride) on her feast day did not disappear when 1 February was re-named St Brigid's Day, and the Corn Goddess is still honoured in Nordic races. 'Educated' people – even those who worship the Mother of God – may believe that such superstition is gone, but in remote rural communities harmless rituals continue as before, and the novels of Thomas Hardy depict them as a living faith in nineteenth-century Britain. Quite recently in surburban Hert-fordshire, a young farmer was seen to stop his combine harves-ter, kneel on the ground and knot the last handful of growing corn into a crude doll![7]

Not all ancient earth deities were female. The Egyptian Geb (Fig 19) grew plants on his back, and one sturdy Babylonian earth god was described as 'Ninurta of the hoe'. Such deities seem to have been helpful and easy-going, expressing perhaps the passive Yin seed within the forward-thrusting Yang mascu-line nature. Lono of Hawaii was the benevolent bringer of healing and forgiveness, but the Roman god Liber was later to be identified with the sensuous Bacchus, earthy indulger of the appetites of the flesh. Many fertility rites, especially in the West, include a man who dresses as a woman. This she-male, as he/she is called, though answering to many another purely local name, often carries a besom broom as an acknowledged

Fig. 19   The earth god Geb lies beneath the vault of heaven formed by his sister Nut, and is separated from her by Shu, the air god and father of them both. Egyptian, c.1000BC. British Museum.

sexual symbol and, despite a grotesque appearance, was originally a solemn attempt at a fusion of the male and female natures. Now merely part of a picturesque country tradition, or a pantomime dame, the she-male once depicted the joining of Sky Father with Earth Mother. A further example of practical cosmic philosophy is found in Tao tradition. Palmer's translation of the *Tung Shu*, the revered, 4000-year-old Chinese Almanac, records that most Chinese homes contained a small, ground-level shrine to the local earth god who, interestingly, represents heavenly power and authority on earth, rights apparently not granted to the Earth Queen in her passive reproductive role.

Animals, too, were worshipped as earth forces or protectors of its sacred gifts. The serpent, often a phallic symbol, represented in many cultures the regenerative energy of the soil and guarded its properties against those who would misuse them. Present in the mythology of all four elements, it is the protective role of the snake which makes its sometimes mysterious appearances more readily understood, for fire, water and air are also the precious supporters of life in this world. It would seem that the serpent stood above all for the continuation of physical fruitfulness.

Fig. 20   The bull adopted as the emblem of John the Evangelist. The signs of the four elements were used as Christian symbols and decorative motifs. Their ooccult significance survives in the twenty-first tarot card, The World. From The Lindisfarne Gospels, *British Library.*

The horse was a vigorous symbol of fertility in Celtic myth and was venerated in huge hill-cut figures. Small statues and carvings of great age have also been found and Bord tells us that rituals involving hobby-horses – some of which still provide seasonal pageantry – originated through that awe. Horned beasts of all kinds suggested sexual power, their phallic-shaped protuberances exciting 'horny' behaviour and often orgiastic ritual. The New Year's Day celebrations of Moldavia still bring out beautifully worked stags' heads attached to embroidered cloths, worn flung over the head in gaudy processions and games. Transformed into wild beasts, human beings could bring out the rampant beast in themselves, and the licentious carnivals of many communities (*carnevale* – farewell flesh) were the pre-Lenten remnants of real generative incitement. Pegg, who finds little basis for belief in dark or even meaningful origins for folk customs, gives two or three pages of his book to describing the almost ritual 'burial' of the man chosen to embody the Spirit of Carnival. The Church may have welcomed this symbolic farewell to flesh, but such vital impregnation of the earth – even by suggestion only – is too closely tied to Bord's theme of divine human sacrifice for it to be trivialized.

Amongst other commonly chosen animal symbols the bull, in particular, signified regeneration and vital strength. In most religions, but not all, these qualities were thought to be housed in the earth. The Cretan bull embodied immense and magic powers, and the incantation of *Ab'rachadab'ra* ('the bull, the only bull'), has invoked them throughout the centuries and is still used in witchcraft.[8] A pagan symbol throughout the East and Middle East, the bull was later to be assigned to the evangelist Luke in a gesture of Christian regeneration. Luke was a physician and the earthiest of the four evangelists (Fig. 20), all of whom were given emblems[9] corresponding to the astrological quarter-markers of Leo – the Lion; Taurus – the bull; Aquarius – the man who carried water; and Scorpio – the eagle's alternative sign.

We must stay with these emblems as they have a direct relationship with the four elements in the context of earth.

Let us look first at a few verses of the vision of Ezekiel:

And I looked, and behold a whirlwind came out of the north, a great cloud, and a fire infolding itself, and a brightness was about it, and out of the midst thereof as the colour of amber, out of the midst of the fire.

Also out of the midst thereof came the likeness of four living creatures. And this was their appearance .... As for the likeness of their faces, they four had the face of a man, and the face of a lion, on the right side: and they four had the face of an ox on the left side; they four also had the face of an eagle.[10]

This vision is interpreted by the Jewish Qabalist[11] Lévi as being an allegory of the world's creation. Chaos of the elements became the four elements cooperating, for the creatures 'stood, and let down their wings'. (Fig. 21) These four beasts, the *cherubim*, were depicted on the front of the Ark of the Covenant.

Fig. 21   The cherubim, four elementary forces in combination. Ezekiel I:10. From The Mysteries of the Qabalah, *by kind permission of the Thorsons Publishing Group.*

The Revelations of John recall Ezekiel's vision, but the four creatures are quite subservient to God and perform no other function but adoration:

. . . and round about the throne were four beasts, full of eyes before and behind.

And the first beast was like a lion, and the second beast was like a calf, and the third beast had a face as a man, and the fourth beast was as a flying eagle.

And the four beasts had each of them six wings about him; and they were full of eyes within: and they rest not day and night, saying, Holy, holy, holy, Lord God Almighty, which was, and is, and is to come.[12]

These biblical references mean more than the harnessing of astrological signs to the will of a creator-God – a concept made plain in the repetition of the 'many eyes' (stars). They also speak of the slave role of the universe. Anthropologist Bernard Campbell does not hesitate to lay blame for the present abused state of the world and its resources on the Judaic duty to be fruitful and multiply. To him it means 'that humankind has come to dominate and subdue nature and today occupies just about every available suitable area of the Earth's surface'. Central to Judaism was the covenant made between God and Abraham: that man was more than an integral, dependent part of nature; that, being made in the image of God, he was able to *behold* the world and form mental and abstract concepts of it; that he was not a victim of it and, indeed, should dominate and interfere. The premise behind what the Jews themselves consider to be the myths of Genesis is that the world is not a self-sufficient network of interconnections and causal law, but a mystery. God, the one and only transcendant Yahweh, is a mystery, and the world is his creation. We shall see that any blame to be imputed for man's current low esteem and low treatment of the natural world must be shared equally amongst all concepts which do not respect the *interaction* of man with his surroundings, and these include their materialistic exploitation by scientists and individuals to whom this earth is far from a mystery.

The Neo-platonists of the first two or three centuries after Christ were concerned about the interconnection of all parts of the universe.[13] They followed up Plato's *Laws* and the theories of the *The Republic* and *Timaeus*, in which he maintained that any causal physical chain originated in the mind of God the Absolute, and that the soul was 'elder-born than all bodies and the prime source of all their changes and transformations'. His idea of the universe as 'an eightfold spindle turning on the knees of Necessity', placed God at the apex in much the same way as the T'ai Chi Absolute (see the diagram in Appendix B), making Plato's concept acceptable to theologians of almost any creed.

The four elements and all they contained circulated in an orderly way beneath the command of a greater intelligence. Huxley has found Neo-platonist doctrines in the traditions and agricultural practices of the Dogon tribe of the Congo, and these were probably implanted by Islamic travellers across the Sahara. Such ideas interested Aquinas, and were combined with Gnostic, Tantric and Hermetic (secret and often magic) philosophies.

Neo-platonist concepts were satisfyingly neat and are still attractive to monotheists, but they permit no divinity to reside within physical matter. Cooper quotes the Neo-platonist Plotinus (c. AD 205–70), whom she considers the supreme philosopher of Western mysticism, as refusing to have his portrait painted, saying, 'Is it not enough to have to bear the image in which nature has wrapped me without consenting to perpetuate the image of an image, as if it were worth contemplating?'

Earthy and material functioning was almost always, to those who seriously 'beheld' man's place in the universe, the lowest aspect of his existence. This book tries in a small way to bolster the interests of the earth element, but it must not be thought that it intends to promote sense-perception beyond its fair one-quarter share of man's concern. Even in those concepts which worshipped qualities of fertility and rebirth, its negative aspects were also constantly noted. Hinduism, which still believes man to be symbolically composed of the four elements of *prakrti*, attributed the plasm of the blood to earth 3000 years ago,[14] and Singh thought that too much of it could lead to over-attachment to material things. Being the most earthbound of the elements, its properties might involve an overbalanced evaluation of the things of earth. Buddhism equates the bodily senses with an ox of clay, and talks of excessive earth clogging the process of enlightenment with doubt: 'Doubting Thomas' epitomizes the down-to-earth nature which must touch and see before it believes.

The Chinese, who invariably divided all concepts into positive and negative aspects, found earthiness to be expressed at times as dullness or lack of imagination, and still suggest gems or emblems to be worn in compensation for the other weak elements, hoping that their qualities will be transmitted. Those who lack the down-to-earth attributes of practicality are advised to wear a piece of stone.[15] As part of his extension of the humoral theory of Pythagoras, Galen expounded on the nature of the cold, dry *Melancholius*, the type of person with too much earth in his bodily system. Sufism calls earth or clay the coarsest matter in the human system, and means by that the body itself. Plato felt the stomach to be the minister of earth needs and rightly situated 'remote from the seat of deliberation' – the brain! And the Gnostics believed all matter to be born of suffering and confusion so that man's spirit yearned to escape its body from the moment it was born.

These ideas slowly made their way to the West and, in medieval Europe, the earthly body was described as 'this piece of earth',[16] 'the centre of my sinful earth',[17] and, in the burial service of 1548, 'earth to earth'. The body and its needs were thus denigrated long before Descartes asseted that they were, in fact, inferior. Though the Zoroastrians preached from 550 BC a reverence for reproduction and earthly fertility, few prophetic religions honour earth processes, since they strive instead to lift the mind and spirit out of the mire of material concern. Paul, we know, abhorred the flesh and its demands. Grimly and frequently he stated that 'they that are in the flesh cannot please God',[18] and only with regret advocated marriage for those who 'cannot contain'.[19]

And yet there remain to us grotesque and often blatantly licentious fertility scenes, not all of which were sculpted, carved, painted or performed during the pre-Christian days of Europe. Bord recounts how a British clergyman had to appear before his bishop for leading a fertility dance round a phallic symbol in 1282,[20] and there are numerous stories of monastic orgies centering on pagan ritual.

Though the early missionaries made dramatic and lasting alterations to pagan sites – St Samson publicly hacking the sign of the cross upon a standing stone in Cornwall[21] – we have only to look at many of our medieval churches, built a thousand years later, to find evidence of earth-power in stones. The phallic symbols and foliate heads, gargoyles and multi-beasts, show a culture not yet divorced from either the fear of preying natural forces or their worship. Many of these carvings are thought to have been copied from designs in the *Physiologus* or

Divine Bestiary, which became popularly used throughout Europe. Barber believes that each contributed a form of symbolic protection from evil, and many were of obvious pagan origin. The seats of the choir stalls in Malvern Priory can be lifted to expose a menagerie of strangely ornamented creatures: they rival the carvings on Kilpeck church for variety, but far surpass them in finger-polished smoothness.

It is only possible to guess at the mentality of a civilization which practises one creed whilst professing another. Yet, seen in universal human terms, it seems plain that such a dichotomy points to an unsatisfying religious faith; one which is not 'speaking to' a certain aspect of human experience. In quite rightly insisting that the things of this world – bodily comforts and provisions of all kinds – would be worthless accompaniments on a spiritual journey, the Church attempted to strip them of all value. Even those who preached against the world and the flesh 'knew' unconsciously that they were denying a human truth. It was truth which their Church's founder had not denied, and the psychic muddle which still exists is probably due to this misunderstanding.

Such a fundamental misunderstanding, which confuses respect for the body (an expression of the self) with a sensual desire for *things*, has largely led to the undervaluing of natural phenomena and functioning today. During the past 400 years Western man's self-esteem has become almost totally dependent on the qualities of his analytical judgement. Told first that his body was a machine and later that he was a progressed ape, not only has his natural ability to perceive the sacred – a watery function – withered,[22] but his cosmic sense has been shamed. The new air religion of dialectical materialism (communism) is largely a kind of fig leaf which attempts to hide the innate disgraces of his nature. This tends to be particularly true in those cultures struggling to throw off the terrorizing effects of voodoo (negative water-fire) religion or social repression. Probably justified to some extent in, for example, some Caribbean and South American cultures, it is less effective in communist countries where surviving ethnic and prophetic 'cults' are clearly not disgraceful or destructive, nor are they inimical to what Engels called measurable and traceable truth.

In spite of the reconciling theories of Teilhard de Chardin and other less respected rebels, by the end of the nineteenth century man was to be described as 'a perambulating tool-box and workshop, fashioned for itself by a very clever piece of slime.'[23] The human body and its senses had been relegated to the status of a measurable thing, to be repaired like a car through surgery, regimented into man-made categories of behaviour and set like a steel-clad robot to sort out the even more inferior world around him. The laws of science had programmed him into this perception of the human role.

Perhaps – though we are not far enough away from those days to tell – it was the colossal suffering brought about by the Great War which was to unsettle European and American attitudes. Perhaps its unprecedented savagery forced a re-appraisal of the route man had chosen for himself. D.H. Lawrence, spokesman for the irrational and instinctive part of man's nature, believer in the direct intuitive response and denouncer of the 'bit and bridle of the intellect', wrote that 'in 1915 the old world ended'.[24]

Did it? The rocket, symbol of modern air-fire technology, is the mascot and apparently the hope of our age. Yet many scientists, conventionally trained within their own disciplines, are calling for a more loving interaction with our bodies and with the natural world. James Lovelock's *Gaia* hypothesis is not a book of folklore but an ecological thesis which suggests that the earth as a whole is a living, organic being. Ian Pearce, amongst other dedicated holistic physicians, believes that each person is a balanced, dynamic energy system, existing on a variety of levels, and interacting with other similar systems in the surrounding environment. Because the earth and all physical matter is Yin – passive, receptive – it *receives*, like the base of the stupa, all the impressions of our other functions. This is true externally: the world around us must endure our despoiling for, although a lack of balance within its own nature – flood, drought, earthquake or hurricane – may temporarily upset its equilibrium, it is not ultimately self-destructive. Man is the destroyer. Earth also *receives* internally, and holistic medicine is based on psychosomatic (psyche-mind, soma-body) principles: that a very large proportion of the diseases from which we suffer are caused by a disrupting emotional state or a faulty attitude of mind.

Earth represented to the ancient world the qualities of fertility, the material nature of the body and its senses, and an unchangingly earthbound psychological outlook. Let us look without prejudice at the functioning of this Yin concept. Earth endures, serves and bears weight: it *becomes* fertilized and can do nothing for or by itself at all. It cannot rise, float, disperse or move; its power lies only in its resilient acceptance and, by itself, it merely exists, solidly. What it lacks in thinking (air), enterprise (fire) or feeling (water), it makes up for by its qualities of comfort, security, caution, service and fertility.

Earth is sensible; it uses the senses and reacts through common-sense (an internal sense which was regarded as the common bond or centre of the five senses). It is above all practical and viable, and these attributes are necessary for human existence in the form of food, clothing, shelter, tools, procreation and all physical comfort. Practical projects require a substantial amount of earthy mental functioning, that is, pragmatic or common-sense evaluation, seeing only material consequences.

People who function strongly in earth tend to be careful, patient, persevering and sensually aware, since psychologically this element confers self-protection, endurance, resilience and sensual evaluation. Their highly developed senses demand satisfaction, and they tend to keep themselves and others well fed and generally looked after. Their preoccupation with earthly comforts may make them materialistic, and may also entail a lack of style or artistic discrimination. Strongly earthy people would rather see well in bright lighting than dream by candlelight, since the senses, not the feelings, are served first. Earthy types invariably prefer the serviceable to the exotic!

Earth triumphs when man caters for his animal needs. Those who are 'unearthed', who value the properties of other elements to the detriment of their animal selves, may suffer in health and in attunement to this world. Their fastidiousness in the face of natural functions, and their squeamish avoidance of encounters with raw (to them brutal – of the brutes) reality, may make human existence almost unendurable. Such people may live largely in the spirit, fasting and neglecting their material appetites, but they are not whole, and probably – like the Gnostics – yearn to be free. The earth function is one quarter of our truth: we must to some extent live in it willy-nilly, but beautified it becomes the symbol of the pastoral dream: archaic man living out in simple dignity his material destiny.

5

The Elements Within

... ther is now at this tyde
As much fyre ayre water y erth as was
Ever before this tyme neither more nor less ....
Remember that thou art compound and create
Of these elements as other creatures be.
  'The Interlude of the Four Elements'. John Rastell, 1510[1]

This is perhaps the place for a brief recap of the traditional meaning of the four elements. If we are to stand in the shoes of Europeans who lived as recently as 300 years ago, we must be very sure of the basis of their education.

Looking at the element itself, we found that the most moderate function of fire was to enlighten. It provided visions, possibilities. A single flame meant that these were encapsulated in one particular ideal. Stronger, thrusting flames represented zeal and drive which might mount to the reckless proportions of an inferno. At this point, fire took control of the other elements in self-assertive, all-consuming activity; it became as disproportionate and out of balance as if it had never been kindled.

The function of water was to bestow a refreshing balance of feeling response. Its mildest form was a light or reflective coating on the other elements, providing a welcome, cleansing shower of gentle caring and feeling. When this began to accumulate in pools or streams, it was possible for a deeper spiritual involvement to take place, but a stream had the added quality of a movement towards the future or towards a great sea mass. It was expressive. Large quantities of water cleaned very thoroughly – purged things – but, if such torrents passed the point of balance, exceeding the quarter-role of each element, they would engulf the other facets of living, ignoring or destroying their reality. This was, indeed, a state of being carried away by feeling, of being as unbalanced as the arid condition of having no feeling at all.

A little air meant that breathing was possible. There could be an exchange of thought. A light and wafting zephyr did not establish anything very clearly, but it prevented a stifling and self-consuming preoccupation with immediate concerns. When air settled into a moderate and balanced breeze, factual matters could be sifted and organized, moved into their correct places and categorized. But if the wind blew up and started jostling the other elements unduly, it might move things which were already quite correctly placed; it could even destroy them. A tornado of mental efficiency made the world just as uncomfortable and out of balance as it would be without a breath of air.

These three elements needed the solid base of earth if they were, themselves, to function in balance. Even a shaky physical foundation would anchor them and give a foundation to which they could relate. In its most meagre presence, earth stabilized the activities of fire and air and gave water a sensible resting-place. If it was of solid dimension, the other elements could better perform their own functions; they could rely on it to support them and to make their efforts real. But if the earth made a bid for supremacy over them, if it cast heavy sods on fire and water and put them out entirely, or enclosed air to stop it moving; if it brought all things down to and into itself, then it deprived the world of all progress and enrichment. Too much earth clogged the works. Too little, and the works did not run smoothly because they were without substance.

It is strange to think that ancestors whose portraits still hang on our walls could look down and know all this without being told. They would probably be of the opinion that this book was yet another scientific or medical textbook! Their own education and culture was based on the European understanding of the four elements of Greek philosophy, and we need to see both its functioning in their lives and the effects of its misunderstanding. For they were us, in no way less genetically evolved and with the same human destiny. And because this study is concerned above all with people and their relationships both with each other and with their world, we are going to look at the concept chiefly as it manifested itself in the four quaint characters of Sanguineus, Colericus, Melancholius and Phlegmaticus.

The idea that air, fire, earth and water might influence – indeed formed – the body and mind, filtered slowly across Europe from the eleventh-century School of Medicine at Salerno. That this practical application found favour with its close neighbour the Vatican was due partly to the Dominican monk Aquinas, who was born in Southern Italy in 1225 and was eventually to become known as the 'angelic doctor'. Although his study of Middle-Eastern and Oriental teachings – which probably included Hermetic theories repugnant to the Church – augmented his beliefs to the point of understanding that the interior workings of the body could affect the soul as well as the mind,[2] his rooted devotion to Christianity made his findings acceptable. We cannot say that Aquinas was responsible for bringing the concept of the four elements to Western Europe, though he visited Britain in 1263, but he succeeded in making it acceptable in the eyes of the Church and thus hastened its spread across Europe.

The Salerno school's teachings, based mainly on the work of Hippocrates and Galen, took hold of the continent, and its textbook was to remain a household guide until the end of the sixteenth century in a system which seems to have been universally appeared. The *Regimen Sanitatis Salernitatum* contained this basic tenet:

> Four humors reign within our bodies wholely,
> And these compared to four elements
> The Sanguine, Choler, Phlegm and Melancholy.[3]

This principle could be accepted on several levels. Most folk neither practised it as a medical theory nor discussed its metaphysical implications. They remained, as it were, chiefly on the receiving end and must have viewed it in much the same way as the psychoanalytic movement of the twentieth century is summed up in, 'He's got a complex about it!' At this trivial level of understanding, the uneducated knew that their behaviour was related to a humor, and the word eventually degenerated into a humour – a mood. Shakespeare, whose writing is full of element symbolism, expressed this through Nym: 'I have an humour to knock you indifferently well.'[4]

We may wonder why this outside knowledge or instruction should prove so instantly welcome to those whose healing had hitherto consisted mainly of witchcraft and a blend of Roman and Celtic herbalism. It may be that it was felt and desired to be true, that a function quite different from the intellect was receiving it into the mind. The overwhelming relief of being able to balance up the elements internally, instead of having to mitigate the evil of hostile external forces, made the elements seem somehow under control. Man *was* the elements, a smaller but proportionate fusion of those same terrifying powers; a microcosm of the macrocosm.

As we know, the concept of the four elements and humors was also abstruse enough for those who, like Aquinas, searched ceaselessly for the ultimate truths about man's physical nature. At its deepest level, scholars encountered the philosophies of the East and the occult Hermetic traditions of the ancient magi. The sixteenth-century Swiss physician 'Paracelsus',[5] respected by Jung as being a forerunner of psychoanalysis, explained through the humoral system a range of human ills, from physical disease through mental functioning to moral weakness and sin. As physician, alchemist, astrologer, neo-Platonist and occult prophet, he sought to redefine man's spiritual nature. The German theosophist Boehme (1575–1624) drew on the Hermetic texts which were collated at that time in Germany[6] and were the basis of the Faust story. Faust was a legendary figure, believed to have lived in Germany and to have died about 1538. He was thought to be a scholar, magician and astrologer, whose taste for evil living led him to make a pact with the devil in return for supernatural aid. Marlowe's *Dr Faustus* told of his passionate desire to manipulate the elements, power he was ultimately denied when Lucifer came to claim his soul. Earth would not gape to hide him, nor could he turn his soul to water drops.

Element control was the obsessive concern of the alchemists and now, stripped of its basis in magic, it is the business of their successors in chemistry. The Hermetic symbols were $\triangle$ (fire) $\underline{\triangle}$ (air) ∇ (water) and $\underline{\nabla}$ (earth). Because it appeared that alchemy set out to challenge the power of God it was frowned upon, but the alchemists saw themselves in many cases as working for God. Thurneisser's *Cabala in Alchemy* (1667) opens with a prayer of preparation of the mind in courage and fortitude.

Even on the most practical level, the application of the humoral system demanded both scholarship and interpretative skills. Every physician needed considerable learning. Astrology, then an observed science and the preoccupation of intelligent minds for at least 2000 years, became integrated with the humoral system, and doctors needed to know planetary positions at the individual's birth before treatment could begin. They then had to choose a precisely favourable hour for treatment and perhaps make a wax talisman which reinforced astrological qualities. Chaucer's Doctor of Physic was

> grounded in astronomye . . ..
> Wel coude he fortunen the ascendant
> Of his images for his pacient.
> He knew the cause of every maladye,
> Were it of hoot or colde, or moyste or drye.

The medical treatise ascribed to Hippocrates and known as the Brussels Astrolabe, stated that no physician was competent without astrological knowledge. Mind and body were thought to be controlled by the complex influence of the zodiac, cosmic forces in which the four elements were of fundamental importance.[7] *The Guildbook of the Barber-Surgeons of York*[8] describes how 'Aries makes the child's head first,' and so on, in correct zodiac order (Fig. 22).

Astrology's teachings came close to earning it harsh treatment from the Church, but its practice was not by itself condemned as heresy, nor counted as witchcraft. Kirby records that Aldhelm studied astrology at the seventh-century ecclesiastical school of Theodore and Hadrian in Canterbury. The Old English *tungel-witega* meant star prophet or sage: astronomy and astrology were one and the same study whose basic premise neither denied the presence of God as controller of the planets and their effects, nor took away man's option to exercise his free will and alter his nature. Jackson and Allen tell us that St Bernadino (1427) preached that planets and constellations govern the body, but that 'the soul is in height and virtue above the whole of the earth, above the water, above fire, above air, above all things which belong to those elements'. This was the

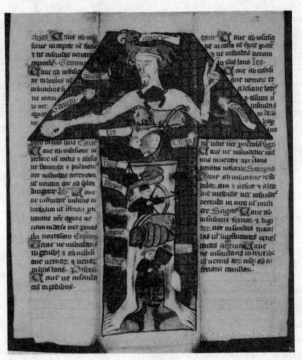

Fig. 22   Table of zodiac influences on the body. Vellum manuscript of 1364, British Library.

Church's stand, and it turned a blind eye to those rich and powerful enough to employ an astrologer, even though they may have sought chiefly the predictive advice which certainly was forbidden. The consultant to Elizabeth I, John Dee, retained the Church's goodwill whilst practising on the very fringes of the occult.[9]

Astrology in medicine centred on the way planetary *principles* reacted with the element *qualities*. The zodiac claims to include in its twelve monthly signs all possible attitudes to, and experiences of, life, each explained in terms of the four elements. Whilst this direct psycho-physical link has never been proved – and we should remember the astro-physicist Sagan's warning that 'absence of evidence is not evidence of absence' – the synthesis appears to have been so efficient that the doctor could often assess at first sight both the patient's disease and the

Fig. 23 The four humoral or elemental types, each recognizable from physique, sin type and behaviour. Note Christ at the centre of the system in this drawing from the fifteenth-century Guildbook of the Barber-Surgeons of York, *British Library.*

celestial influence most likely to make him succumb to it. His *complexion* (meaning a twinning together) would provide the clue.

The most noble complexion consisted of equal quantities of all four humors, but the usual *temperament* (mixing in proportions) suggested a preponderance of one or at most two, which gave the individual a characteristic appearance. (as shown in Figs. 23 and 25) This would be modified by planetary influences, but again these conferred particular and recognizable physical features. The humoral and planetary disposition also suggested a likely way of behaving and tendencies towards certain preoccupations; these are shown symbolically in the four humoral 'types' of Figs. 23 and 25. In the first of these, an illustration from *The Guildbook of the Barber-Surgeons of York,* a work still in use in the reign of Charles I, shows the head of Christ placed at the centre of the system, embodying, perhaps, the facial features and skin type of a perfectly balanced temperament. The scrolls read: 'There are the four humors . . . granting th(is) kind of use . . . they are referred unto the four elements . . . they are otherwhiles called the four complexions.

The second, a German woodcut, has carefully planted the feet of each character in the appropriate element! The accompanying scrolls are printed in Latin, but German handscript notes the humoral qualities – 'cold and dry' and so on – alongside each figure. Latin was the language of the educated, and no textbooks (including the Bible) were printed in the vernacular in early medieval Europe[10] so, by retaining the Latin name for each type, we shall preserve both the official medical term and its universal European meaning.

Sanguineus was ruled by air but, although generally admired, he was seldom encountered, (according to my sources). Physically he was alert and comely, with soft pink skin and fine fingernails. The ancient study of cheirology – of Chinese origin and by the Middle Ages already 3000 years old – found the temperament to be concentrated in the hands, whose appearance seemed to imply hereditary tendencies. This theory is not as far-fetched as it may sound. The brain, the nervous system, the sense organs and the skin are all derived from the ectoderm of the embryo at the same time, so it is not particularly surprising that the hands and fingers, being in close contact with these vital centres, should reflect internal conditions. The hands are an obvious choice for psycho-physical study. No other single organ of the body receives such vast quantities of information from the brain, and Watson has suggested that, if human proportions were determined only by nerve supply, we should all have hands the size of beach umbrellas! Modern physicians are taught to recognize signs of illness or propensity towards specific diseases – such as clubbing of the fingers in cardiac disease[11] – and several doctors have been sufficiently interested in these phenomena to make a special study of them.[12]

To return to Sanguineus, the airy type. His hands would be lean, with skinny, knotty fingers set squarely on the palm, as opposed to the sloping effect seen on other types. They might have spatulate (squared-off) tips, and the palm would be square. Medieval cheirologists were tied to Galen's theory of Hot Moistness, but modern students believe the airy person to have cool and inflexible hands. (Fig. 24)

Sanguineus's mind – and the mind of the air type is his strength – was subtle and penetrating, but likely to move on quickly if he became bored. The same tendency applied to his relationships with the opposite sex! Irrepressibly freedom-loving, he liked distractions; 'anything which made one jump for joy'.

Now this description, from a French text of 1620 by du Moulin, is of what we should call an extrovert. It could also be said to refer chiefly to the mutable (adaptable) air sign of Gemini whose subjects, ruled by Mercury, are traditionally versatile, quick-thinking and flirtatious – thinkers of a more superficial nature than Librans (cardinal, active air) or Aquarians (fixed air). Du Moulin noted that strong Mercury influence would give the sanguine type good judgement and a 'public voice' although by nature studious, he had a taste for projects, a word which means to 'throw forward', and is concerned with creative, exteriorized thinking.

Because astrology, like cheirology but unlike the humoral system, is a living synthesis, the present tense is used throughout this chapter when discussing its interpretation of the signs and elements. The past tense is only used when quoting the effects of planetary influence from medieval sources, when they

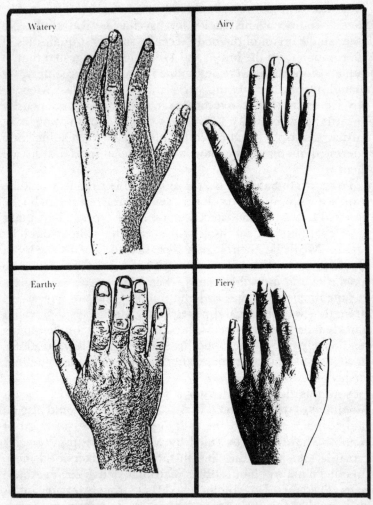

Fig. 24   Element influences seen in handshapes. Pure 'types' are seldom found, but element characteristics are often obvious. Line drawings adapted from photos by J.G-W.

were treated as underlying causes of the complexion.

Still with the air type, we meet Libra, the sign ruled by Venus. The symbol of Libra is the scales, and its subjects are said to arbitrate and deliberate endlessly, thinking problems through in their search for equilibrium. Aquarius the water-carrier deals in air-waves, brain-waves. As we have already heard, he is thought to collect the waters of wisdom and pour them out again for the benefit of mankind; his airy nature is a blend of sharp intellectual perception and deep comprehension. Unlike Libra, who seeks a partner, he shares Sanguineus's detached avoidance of emotional entanglement! But let no one suppose that these definitions refer solely to sun signs: no reputable astrologer of either the Middle Ages or the present day would stand by such a scanty appraisal. Both would be talking of air qualities assessed from the entire birth chart.

Boehme, looking at this type from a theosophical standpoint, emphasized the mental arrogance of those with an over-airy nature, a view borne out by the later attempts of the intellect to account for all man's responses. Paracelsus likened the airy type to sylphs, the denizens of air, who needed to learn constancy.[13] Pope's eighteenth-century *Rape of the Lock* lampooned this concept, but we note his introductory preference for the sylphs, as being 'the best-conditioned creatures imaginable'.

Colericus suffered in reputation through his psycho-physical links, for Fire and its effects were still dreaded in medieval Europe. The classic type had hot, dry, hard skin and thick black fuzzy hair. His eyes were deep and bitter, as was his mouth; he had a small head, large chest and a penetrating, resonant voice. He walked quickly, was rowdy and argumentative in public, would not 'speak to order' and showed anger without hesitation. He slept little and, when he did, had nightmare visions of fires, flames and murders. Actually, he much preferred to spend his time in bed in other activities! His character was saved by his honesty, warm heart, courage, liberal giving, willingness to learn and the ease with which, in spite of his hot temper, he could be placated. The ascendant or rising sign of Colericus was crucial because this governed his manner and behaviour, sometimes masking the fiery rulership within. Du Moulin adds that a bad aspect with Saturn would make the choleric type weepy and depressed, with lowered eyes, increased sleeplessness and lack of appetite.

The many other planetary influences described in Du Moulin's *Vraye et Parfaicte Chiromancie et Phisionomie* made the physician's diagnosis a matter of complex equation, and the three fiery types of the zodiac differed themselves in nature.

Fig. 25   German woodcut showing the four humoral or elemental types. Note that the feet of each 'type' are set in the appropriate element. Stadtbibliothek, Zurich.

The cardinal (active) fire of Aries is the most directly thrusting and least controlled, flaring with a self-assertion as of right. Named in ancient Greece after Ares the war-god – though the 'ram' sign is far older – this type has the nature of a crusader. His will, dynamism and fearlessness is signified by a sword (Fig. 25), but his choleric temper burns out fast. In contrast, Leo's fixed fire burns with a strong and steady flame. His lion-proud dignity assumes authority and distinction and, although a sunny nature usually prevails, thunder clouds gather if he is patronized, given orders or exposed to others' achievements. The adaptable fire of Sagittarius both scorches and enlightens: the archer shoots his arrows of searing wisdom towards a far horizon, ignoring the petty concerns beneath his swift-galloping hooves, and his fiery darts more closely resemble the intuitive flame of John Donne (see p. 24), than the dynamic force of Colericus.

Paracelsus likened the fire type to a salamander, the creature supposed to dwell in fire, and believed his life's lesson to be the learning of placidity. Boehme saw anger and passion as his chief failings – hellish flames which gave the choleric his fearsome reputation. The *new humoralism* of Gaub, one book of which was still in use well into the nineteenth century, had this to say of the fire-dominated:

> You will praise the pungent spirit and glowing imagination, the fiery readiness for action and the steadfastness of the choleric man, but you will deplore the ready rashness to dare all, and the harsh irascibility and insufferable pride with which they are coupled.

The public image of the fire-brand has now improved to the point where 'fire in the belly' is considered an important asset. (Sadly, we shall come to realize, this active and assertive feature of the West has reacquired in the East many of the brutal qualities of the ancient fire gods, and is in danger of becoming once more the most worshipped of all deities.) In its negative aspect fire destroys and consumes, yet the fire qualities of Colericus are always capable of positive good.

In the hands, these qualities are thought to show in long palms, shortish fingers and, particularly, flexible and elastic movements. Most striking is their flame shape, created by the curved sides of the palm and outside fingers. (Fig. 24) The hard redness of the forceful innovator recalls the Hot Dryness of Galen, but creative imagination gives a soft pinkness and a typically conic hand known to cheirologists as the *psychic*.

Slow and passive behaviour was the hallmark of *Melancholius*, the earthy member of the humoral quartet. He was thought to have cold, dry, rough skin, hard bones and a liverish temperament which showed in his sallow skin. His hands were square with short, blunt fingers, and had an appearance of strength. Aquinas referred to the coarse-textured hands of those without clear understanding,[14] but modern cheirologists remind us of the precise skills or artistic abilities of these useful, tool-using hands. They point out that, although they may be weathered by work, they are just as frequently beautifully soft, like fine chamois leather. But the skin tends to be noticeably thick and dense and, though no cheirologist would now refer to it as blackish or greenish – terms presumably used in the Middle Ages to recall black bile influence! – it has now been described as 'sun tanned', having the general appearance of outdoor health.[15]

Melancholius was believed to become prematurely old and white-haired. He was avaricious (Fig. 25) and distrustful of his friends, a failing noted by Boehme and depicted by Paracelsus in the earthy gnome who needed to learn cheerful generosity. Apart from occasional outbursts of rage he was slow to anger, nor was he luxurious in his habits. He was seldom excited by the opposite sex.

Du Moulin noted that a predominant placing of the moon in Melancholius's horoscope made him corpulent. (The addition of a watery element to an earthy one is likely to bog it down, slowing down productive movement and increasing placidity.) The influence of Mars made him lazy – this is difficult to explain – and turned him into an insulter. It also gave him a marked face, a disfigurement also said by du Moulin to be conferred by strong Saturn influence.

These qualities are not entirely reflected in the cardinal (active) earth of Capricorn, the zodiac sign ruled by Saturn. Sometimes described as the god of decay, this planet is actually thought to confer discipline, restraint and responsibility. In practice, it seems to provoke pessimism and anxiety, as was shown by its effects on Colericus. Because they lack abstract hope, Capricornians admire substantiated work and concrete results; and their sexuality, like other forms of generosity and relating, only blossoms when they see success spread before their eyes. This kind of earthiness achieves low-profile but undeniable success and, though Capricorn subjects are often little old people when young, their plodding efforts often bring self-satisfied contentment in the end.

Very different is the Venus-ruled Taurean. The bull symbolized earth-power, fertility and growth, and this spring-time sign embodies qualities of sensual enjoyment and love of luxury. All earth types have a liking for harmonious stability, but this sign's earthy resilience can turn into stubbornness. The rare and alarming attacks of the thoroughly aroused bull are capable of demolishing the forces of all the other zodiac signs, and rulership of Taurus is believed by one astrologer rightly to belong to the predicted but as yet unidentified planet Apollo.[16]

Virgo – mutable earth – signifies the Earth Mother goddess, but in many respects characterises an old maid! The sign is ruled by Mercury and this perceptibly airy influence makes Virgo hyper-critical, with a pedantic assurance of opinion. Qualities of resilient endurance typify all the earth signs, but here precision in material matters is paramount.

Like the other three elements, weak earth can be strengthened in any individual. There is little doubt that we are not all born with the same aptitudes and those, in particular, who boast of slender, limp hands far removed from the robustness of the broad, tool-using australopithicine,[17] may indeed feel that they live more in the spirit than in matter. The water nature, linked with the earthy in the Yin aspect of the T'ai Chi and basically passive, has little of the stolid endurance of earth.

The medieval *Phlegmaticus*, ruled as he was by the phlegma of his system and under the constant influence of the moon, had cold, moist, fleshy skin, straight veins and a thin chest. Du Moulin also observed that he was relatively hairless and with scant beard. The meaning of *phlegmatic* has changed over the centuries – to the extent that many people wrongly take it as an earthy quality – in the same way that sanguine now implies optimistic hopefulness. We must think of Phlegmaticus as ruled by tidal waves of impressionability, and belonging to that end of the human spectrum least equipped to deal with the harsher side of life.

While the earthy hand seems to possess an extra, protective layer of skin, the water hand appears to lack a skin or two, for it is translucent and vulnerably naked. Straight veins suggest the easy flow of fluid, and Hartleib describes this absence of obstruction as allowing the intuitive flow to reach the fingertips and thus to extend to others. The hands of healers may express this quality. Watery fingers are round and smooth, plump in appearance whatever their owner's build. On a truly phlegmatic hand they should be long and pointy-tipped, the shape so loved by artists, with soft, fine-textured skin. Pre-Raphaelite paintings suggest the influence of Venus which confers extreme whiteness, and of Jupiter which adds beautiful hair and pleasing manners, but hands of this idealistic type are rarely seen.

Being receptive and impressionable, Phlegmaticus was more vulnerable than any other type to planetary influences and took on their qualities with visible clarity. The moon gave him a moon face, round and bland and with large soft eyes. Mars conferred upstanding hair and a reddish or yellowish tinge to the complexion. Because he drifted according to whichever current pushed him most forcefully, Phlegmaticus was likened by Paracelsus to an *undine*, a watery creature which, above all, needed to learn firmness. The three water signs of the zodiac are powerfully coloured by their respective rulers and convey quite different aspects of feeling awareness. Pisces, mutable (adaptable) water, is ruled by Neptune, and so represents the qualities of submerged response. Its cloudy and mystical obscurity may be expressed in one of two ways – a choice symbolized by the fishes of its glyph: one faces the world with flowing charity, while the other recoils from its demands. The Piscean inclination to dulling its sensitivity with alcohol or drugs was unsympathetically ascribed in the Middle Ages to the cold wetness which sapped energy: Phlegmaticus was believed to have no desire for sexual activity unless warmed and filled with wine – a cold fish indeed. Yet the profound depths of the Pisces nature enable him to transcend human experience in a scarcely conscious state of spirituality.

The moon-ruled Cancer receives through its cardinal (active) water the emotional states of others, but its response can vary from a soothingly warm bath to a coldly enveloping wet blanket! Influenced in an almost tidal way by his moods, Cancer can certainly be 'crabby', projecting the qualities of envy and resentment noted by Boehme; but he fulfils his nature best by protective sentiment. His is not the clear, *fixed* water of Scorpio whose charge of intense feeling is given qualities of regeneration and refinement by its ruler, Pluto. This sign is doubly intuitive, its water galvanized by the fiery Mars which was, until 1934, believed to be its ruler; but its fixed properties hold it in check so that it remains largely passive, achieving power through its purging.

The qualities of water-consciousness were ill-appreciated by exponents of the humoral system. The German Gaub, while writing treatises on such psychosomatic topics as 'Death from Unshed Tears', dismissed them ruthlessly: 'Shall I arouse the sleepy phlegmatics, unresponsive to everything, striving greatly for nothing, of whom it may be said that they live for their guts and bellies alone?'

His use of the word unresponsive is particularly interesting, showing the eighteenth-century predilection for action and articulate expression, the exteriorizing of feeling. We know, of course, that responding is exactly what the water-dominated do best but, to the contemporaries of Gaub, responding meant reacting visibly and producing reflected expressions of that inner feeling.

Gaub is making an important observation, one which recalls the emphasis placed by Boehme on the envious nature of Phlegmaticus. Impotent, unexpressed feeling – like envy – is always destructive but, because the water type is so predominantly involved (physically as well as mentally) in his emotional awareness, repression may truly 'kill' him. Modern research into such diseases as cancer suggests that destruction may be literal since, although some physical interactions may be inevitable, their rate of increase may be governed by mental attitudes.[18] Gregory (of Egyptian birth), recalls the belief in ancient Egyptian medicine that illness could be cured by the herb, the knife and the word. The wide-ranging power of this third instrument embraces all forms of psychosomatic treatment, and is a consideration of the human being in his wholeness. We shall see that holistic medicine came to be so named because, for a long time, the knife and the herb (drugs) ignored the less obvious claims of spiritual sickness.

The ordering of the elements into a physical, mental and spiritual pattern made them at least in part friends and allies, and there were few areas of medieval living which did not include a working knowledge of the nature of the elements. As the undisputed basis of all matter they were the subject of works which stressed that humanity's interaction with nature was not one of domination on either side. The dramatic arts had been born in Europe through religious tableaux inside churches and in the streets, and the tradition of making moral points in plays has continued. Many medieval interludes and masques were blatant preaching, and John Rastell's *Interlude of The Four Elements*, a verse from which headed this chapter, was a cross between a morality play and a science lesson. Through its characters and dialogue Rastell tried to emphasize that the external elements worked with man and not against him, and that patterns in nature – such as tides and variable climates – were beneficial to him and not intended as a threat.

This deeper understanding of the elements allayed much deep-rooted fear and began to bring about the acceptance of the greater physical world, probably contributing to the intrepid adventuring and colonization of the sixteenth century. The whole of Europe burgeoned into optimistic confidence during this period, leaving splendid tributes to its collective mentality.

It was to be centuries before the system of the four humors or elements disappeared completely from medical textbooks. To this day the Mars/Venus, male/female symbols are retained: $\male$ $\female$. Long after Vesalius (1514–64) flouted the laws of the Church and opened the human body with a knife, thus allowing anatomical study, the idea of man as a microcosm of the macrocosm remained. In 1600 Harvey dismissed Galen's theory that the blood ebbed and flowed like the tide and, gradually, his other teachings fell into disuse, but the four-humor concept, with its basic idea of cosmic unity and inter-action, was slow to die. We shall find that those parts of it which survived, despite the findings of anatomy, were supported by reasoned and observed (empirical) evidence.

Robert Burton's *Anatomy of Melancholy* (1628) ranged over all known medical practice, and compared the effects of the four external elements, viz., 'the best soil yields the worst air'. Thomas Sydenham, a celebrated doctor of the mid-seventeenth century, foreshadowed later knowledge by finding the humors to be susceptible to particles in the atmosphere, and reaffirmed that disease was due to 'fermentations or putrefactions of the humors'. But 100 years later Gaub's series of dissertations still centred on the premise that 'the composition of the solid and fluid components of the human body, as well as the course of the natural and vital functions, differ in the different temperaments'.

Glaub extended the theory of humors into many areas which are the subject of 'original' discovery today, and all of which stressed the interdependence of body and mind. His papers included *Beneficial Corporeal Effects of Joy, Faith and Love, The Harmful Corporeal Effects of Suppressed Anger on the Body* and *Harmful Corporeal Effects of Terror.*

The cold wind of change introduced by Descartes and his followers removed a great deal of what had become an assumed harmony between spirit and flesh, and caused ridicule and scorn to be heaped upon venerable metaphysical concepts. Among the first to be swept away were the ancient and totally unsubstantiated claims to scientific knowledge of astrology. Banished from university curricula, the study became almost extinct in Europe but was preserved and practised in Britain. The diarist Pepys respected William Lilly, a renowned astrologer and his friend, and did not care for the cutting protrait of him as 'Sidrophel' in Samuel Butler's *Hudibras* of 1662.[19] The later centuries of the age of reason were to categorize astrology as superstition and its predictions as pernicious folly, but these few lines from *Hudibras* sum up its rejection:

> [He] with the Moon was more familiar
> Than e'er was almanack well-willer.
> Her secrets understood so clear,
> That some believ'd he had been there.
> Knew when she was in fittest mood
> For cutting corns or letting blood,
> When for annointing Scabs or Itches
> Or to the Bum applying leeches;
> When Sows and Bitches may be spade,
> And in what Sign best cider's made . . . .

The four humors of medicine were believed to have some basis in physical theory and lingered on, as we have seen, in much orthodox practice. But the psychological qualities so long associated with them had no place in a human mind which loftily relegated the senses and feelings, and words like 'fiery' and 'earthy' became detached from their psycho-physical origins. Intellectuals who came across esoteric texts concerning man's place in the universe mocked them mercilessly; the elemental beings of Paracelsus, for example, became pawns in Pope's *Rape of the Lock*:

> For when the Fair in all their Pride expire,
> To their first elements their Souls retire;
> The Sprights of fiery Termagents in Flame
> Mount up, and take a Salamander's name.
> Soft yielding minds to water glide away,
> And sip, with Nymphs, their Elemental Tea.
> The graver Prude sinks downward to a Gnome,
> In search of mischief still on earth to roam.
> The light coquettes in Sylphs aloft repair,
> And sport and flutter in the fields of Air.

Pope learned of the elementals through the Rosicrucian *Compte de Gabalis* writings, a French book which, in spite of Pope's comment that it was like a novel, contained much Hermetic lore. Huxley quotes the satirical lampooning of its circulating elements in Cyrano de Bergerac's comic skit, 'States and Empires of the Moon'. The argument centres on a log of wood and, hilarious though it may have been in 1875, its scientific flaws do not disguise the unchanging laws of nature; the passage points an accusing finger at the nineteenth century rather than at *Le Compte de Gabalis*. Roughly translated, it states that latent fire within the log is liberated by the striking of a match. This forces out the elemental moisture (sap), while moist particles of fire rise into the sky and are lost in the clouds. The log's air turns into clouds and, when it rains, fire and air return to the earth. The log has now turned to ash which is a kind of earth cured of its sterility by fire. An acorn, dropped in this ash and watered by rain containing fire and earth, grows into a tree which can once more be consumed by, and reborn from, the same process.

This kind of thinking was knocked flat by scientific certainty.

It was simply no longer possible to take a philosophical view of matters whose truth could be established under bright laboratory lights, and the nineteenth century saw the beginning of the end of blended, comprehensive study. In 1880 the Metaphysical Society was dissolved because specialized interests and polarities of opinion had made inter-disciplinary discussion unworkable.[20] The date marks not only the closing of an era but the lowest ebb so far in the cooperation of the different functions of man's nature. From that point, until the gradual dissemination of holistic ideas in the second half of the twentieth century, Europeans have pigeonholed and divorced the separate aspects of existence and, though the word *holism* was coined in 1926 by J.C. Smuts, its meaning is still not widely understood.

The quaintness and misunderstandings of the humoral system – not to mention some of the bloodcurdling measures taken to restore bodily equilibrium[21] – do not make the entire concept outdated rubbish. The *new humoralists* of the late 1800s, led by Brown-Séquard and Bernard, talked of an internal homeostat,[22] and the holistic medicine of the present day includes that premise. I am not suggesting that we should re-learn the humoral system, but that we might benefit from its attempts at balancing four very different but equally important elements. The dualists' dictum that the mind of man was greater than his surroundings, and that he must now relinquish his notions of integration with the cosmos and instead set about subduing, is not ultimately a healthy one, and it may be that we can retrace our steps a little from the wrong turning we have taken.

6

In Our Element

... But that, so much of earth and water wrought,
I must attend time's leisure with my moan;
Receiving nought by elements so slow
But heavy tears, badges of either's woe:

The other two, slight air and purging fire,
Are both with thee, wherever I abide;
The first my thought, the other my desire,
These present-absent with swift motion slide.
For when these quicker elements are gone
In tender embassy of love to thee,
My life, being made of four, with two alone
Sinks down to death, oppress'd with melancholy.

Shakespeare Sonnets XLIV and XLV

Modern man, searching still for reasons and proof, is sometimes humbled by the wisdom of those who lived before him: without much recourse to libraries or museums they appeared to have made the same discoveries as himself but to have achieved a deeper understanding of them. Such a seeker was C.G. Jung.

Not only had this twentieth-century doctor (1875–1961) lasting respect for the thinkers of past ages, but he also believed that the memories and impressions of our forebears are still contained in the 'vast historical storehouse'[1] of our unconscious mind. European and American philosophers had made considerable inroads into what came to be called the study of the unconscious before Sigmund Freud applied scientific principles to it;[2] but Freud (1856–1939) did not go beyond the boundaries of the individual's own relationships in relating disorders of the mind to past experience. His dissident pupil Jung asked more: that man not only look downwards and inwards to find out the truth about himself, but also backwards 'into the depths of time and down into the labyrinth of the physiological continuum'.[3]

Jung believed that many of our ideas and, in particular, the subject matter of our dreams, had 'been stamped on the human brain for aeons'.[4] He used *fourness*, the tendency to divide all aspects of life into four divisions, as an example of a concept which played a great role in many religions and philosophies and which may be unconsciously familiar to us all.[5] He referred to it in *Psychology and the East:*

> If we study, for instance, the introspective method of medieval natural philosophy, we find that it repeatedly used the circle, and in most cases the circle divided into four parts, to symbolise the central principle, obviously borrowing this idea from the ecclesiastical allegory of the quaternity as found in . . . the four evangelists, the four rivers of paradise, the four winds, and so on.

Jung drew inspiration from many of the cultures and religious beliefs we have touched upon, amongst them Taoism, Hinduism, Buddhism, Gnosticism, Neo-platonism and the Hermetic and Qabalic traditions. They augmented his clinical experience in the creation of his four *Psychological Types*, but he gave these fresh and independent form and avoided comparisons with older 'types' of behaviour. He found the four temperaments of Galen 'superficial from the psychological standpoint, since they dealt only in external appearances'.[6]

Nevertheless, the imagery he used in describing his Types makes them inseparable from the main theme of our study. In his 1934 Tavistock lectures Jung referred to the Coptic *Codex Brucianus* and its analogy of the Son of God as 'a city with four gates . . . which symbolises the idea of totality; it is the individual who possesses the four gates of the world, the four psychological functions . . .'.[7]

Jung also acquired a profound understanding of the relationship between man and the external elements, perhaps most beautifully expressed in *Psychology and the East*. Late in life he spoke of his country childhood amongst animals and peasants, and the 'full consciousness' it had given him, a consciousness which eludes town-dwellers but may be accessible through psychoanalysis.[8] But he did not directly link the elements to the Types, nor the Types to the four medieval humors, though similarities are very clear.

His concern lay with the four functions of the mind and their interaction within the individual. His ideal, towards which he worked with his patients, was to integrate the four functions and bring them all into consciousness, and he called this 'making whole of the psyche' *individuation*. However, and we need to know this before considering the nature of the four functions and their relationship to one another, Jung did not 'believe that it is humanly possible to differentiate all four functions alike, otherwise we would be perfect like God, and that will surely not happen'.[9]

For Jung the difficulty of individuation lay chiefly in the irreconcilable nature of certain of the functions. In this he stood alone: no other philosophy or creed states that any two functions (elements) *cannot* cooperate.

Let us look at Jung's psychological types and the way they interact. These are his own definitions;[10] the bracketed elements are my addition.

Sensation (sense perception) tells you that something exists (Earth);

Thinking tells you what it is (Air);

Feeling tells you whether it is agreeable or not (Water);

Intuition tells you whence it comes and where it is going (Fire).

Although Jung had 'no desire to give readers the impression that such pure types occur at all frequently in actual practice',[11] he generally found that, in most people, one of the four functions tended to correspond with the most obvious means by which the conscious self adapted to the world. This *principal* or dominant function would confer a characteristic way of behaving.[12] Here are some extreme examples of my own choosing which should make this clear:

Principal function, *sense perception or sensation* (the earthy Doubting Thomas);

Principal function, *thinking* (the airy René Descartes);

Principal function, *feeling* (the watery William Wordsworth);

Principal function, *intuition* (the fiery John Donne).

Jung used the term intuition to mean solely active, innervating intuition, that is, stimulation through the nerves. (Intuition means the obtaining of knowledge instantly, bypassing the thinking or reasoning processes; it can correctly be applied to both water and earth functioning, therefore, in addition to Jung's obviously fiery definition. Intuition is clearly defined in Appendix C.)

Note, too, that Jung's description of the intuitive type does not include fire in the sense of drive or force. For Jung this aspect of behaviour was a quality of the *libido* which expressed psychic energy.[13] In all other respects his extroverted, intuitive type corresponds to the fiery Colericus, as the characteristics described in *Psychological Types* reveal. The astrologer Liz Greene, who is also a Jungian psychologist, prepared this compass which harmonizes the types and the elements.* [14]

We can learn from this compass that because Jung stipulated that it could only revolve, putting a different function in the position of principal (at the top) according to each individual,

* Reproduced from *Relating* by kind permission of Thorsons Publishing Group.

the two opposing functions could never combine. There could be no 'intuitive sensation' or 'feeling thought', for instance. Jung believed that each principal function necessarily had its opposite (see diagram), which would remain poorly developed and in an archaic or unconscious state. This function would be badly expressed by the individual who would scarcely understand its nature and would probably resent it when well expressed by other people. (The hooliganism mentioned at the end of chapter 3 is an example of unconscious air function resulting in hostility.)

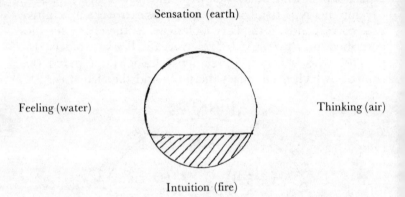

Sensation (earth)

Feeling (water)　　　　　　　　　　　　　　　　　Thinking (air)

Intuition (fire)

The two functions on the side of the compass were *auxiliary* or supported the principal function; one was probably more consciously used than the other.

Jung's insistence that two opposite functions could not consciously cooperate does not appear to be consistently valid. 'People who go by feeling-values leave thinking well alone', he said, 'And they are right to do so.'[15] This book respectfully differs from Jung on that point. We shall find many instances later on of splendid harmony between 'opposites'. The counsellor, for example, uses thinking and feeling in equal conscious measure, and the artist conveys with practical and material skill the vision within his mind. This is also true of those with dynamic ideas and the practical common-sense to put them to work: the entrepreneur functions consciously in both sensation and intuition and is embodied in the 'steam-roller' of fire-earth symbolism. But on many occasions the weakest function of the individual does correspond to the darkened area of Jung's compass.

Before we leave this important psychological theory, we must understand that, in truth, Jung depicted not four but eight psychological types. Each function on the compass was either 'extroverted' or 'introverted', terms which Jung invented but which were inspired by the T'ai Chi symbol of Yin and Yang opposites. The words are so frequently misused that we shall be using them as little as possible; in any case they refer to functions and attitudes and not to people, few of whom fail to show extroverted tendencies when at home, or have not withdrawn into themselves in the face of intimidating new circumstances. Jung himself found the terms too 'superficial and general', and their inadequacy led him to 'find some further basic peculiarities' – his psychological types.[16]

The French psychologist Ania Teillard studied under Jung; her imaginary dinner party of the eight 'types' imprints them on the memory. They are, of course, so exaggerated as to be almost *archetypes* – prototypes. The difficult dinner party continues despite the absence of Introverted Intuitive who has forgotten he was invited and is wandering along the banks of the Seine on a freezing night without a coat, stopping every so often to read another page of his book!

The entire Western world is in Jung's debt not only for his theory of types, but for his introduction of Eastern, Middle-Eastern, medieval and esoteric wisdom – and I use the word 'wisdom' carefully, for we do not mean *knowledge* – into the study of the human mind. Though the I Ching, an ancient Chinese method of divination, told him that its wisdom would be unappreciated in Europe, indeed that it would represent 'a deep and dangerous waterhole in which one might easily be bogged down', his response was that 'the thoughts of the old masters are of greater value to me than the philosophical prejudices of the Western mind'.[17] He impelled twentieth-century Europe to look to the past and to the far side of the world, 'where people have trained their minds in introspective psychology for thousands of years, whereas we began with our psychology not even yesterday but only this morning'.[18]

We have not heard the last of Jung in this study. Its theme is closely tied to the mainspring of his inspiration and his views

must intrude from time to time, although they are not necessarily in agreement with what is said. It is believed by some
psychologists that Jung's four psychological types dwindled in
appeal because they were encased in rigid theory: psychother-
apists could not make their clients conform to type, and there
was no way of applying the principles of his functions unless
they did. By referring constantly to the interaction of our minds
with the four elements of nature, I have attempted to remove
the concept from the bounds of psychoanalysis and set it at the
disposal of all those – whether of open mind or closed discipline
– who have a right to speak on it. And that is all of us.

It is, as the ancient Greeks promised, possible to see all things
in terms of the four elements and our consciousnesses may
suggest extraordinary and bizarre applications. They are all
valid. But for the moment we are going to look only at the four
mental functions and predispositions of the human mind and
see how they affect our behaviour.
   I am not offering a typology, believed by Mayr and others to
be incompatible with evolutionary thinking. (In fact, several
syntheses of the four elements already exist and are referred to
in the course of this book.) We are looking only at functions and
attitudes. We are seeing ourselves as we stand in the here and
now; twentieth-century beings fashioned – according to the
ideas of our time – by our genes, our personal history, cultural
conditioning and oft-changing environment.[19] No one can
predict what the inter-response of organism and environment
will be: no one can tell how much our conditioning will affect
our perception of the world. The self at the centre of these
influences cannot be reduced to argument, but a great deal can
be learned about the separate features of that self.
   The caricatures of Colericus, Melancholius, Sanguineus and
Phlegmaticus helped to depict familiar human attitudes, and
the four historical figures chosen by me to depict Jung's
psychological types created visual images of an abstract concept. The medieval characters showed contemporary prejudice
and, sadly, we still adopt critical attitudes towards mentalities
not our own. We are bound to recognize acquaintances in the
images which follow, but can we be sure that we shall see
ourselves? Hui-Neng, sixth patriarch of Zen Buddhism, urged

a clearing of all impulse to pre-judge: 'Think not of good, think not of evil, but see what at the moment your own original features are . . . .'[20]

The way the elements work within our own mind is best shown through some common, everyday experiences. These make it easy to see how misunderstandings and conflicts arise, and they may point clearly towards a bias in our perception: we may constantly find ourselves identifying with the attitudes of one or two particular elements and disliking one of the others intensely. On the other hand, we may find that no pattern emerges and that our choices of attitudes are mixed or blurred. This may mean that we are well balanced but, on the other hand, it may not. It may mean that none of our elemental functions is fully conscious!

Looking for features and functions in our attitudes increases self-knowledge, but I am not suggesting that anyone should spend very long over it. Self-conscious man cannot become self-aware through deliberate (conscious) effort; he can only expose himself to ideas which may release his awareness, and that for a short time. Having learned a little about himself, he will then turn more happily to something in which he can forget himself. The value of considering these elemental attitudes lies in our own response to them, which may be very surprising indeed if it reveals facets of our nature of which we were completely unaware.

We begin where we are; where we live. Few of us are able to live exactly where we choose but there is usually a small amount of choice and in particulars, we can be remarkably adamant. We choose our friends to complement our strengths to harmonize with our natures; we adapt even temporary lodgings to suit them. Children are often quick to point out the ways in which they would alter their homes to suit their natures!

Earthy people like to live close to animals and reality. Their gardens are useful and probable well maintained, but they may not be beautiful and may be cluttered with chattels which might be useful. Comfort and convenience always come first and attention is regularly paid to this aspect of home life. The kitchen is a very important room and strongly earthy people would rather invest in the housekeeping than in the house.

Earthy natures prefer low-lying land and Arroyo points out that they often choose bungalows.

The watery need for feeling and human warmth produces a nest-like atmosphere, family photographs and exposed intimacies. Radio, telephone and television are needed for human contact, but cannot take the place of loved people. Old or previously inhabited buildings are preferred and, for choice, water-predominant individuals do not care to live in isolated positions. They are drawn to places near water. If the watery nature is a profoundly spiritual one, the house will resemble a shrine or hermitage.

Air has no need for a secure foundation and airy folk do not look for old buildings. A place for paperwork, reading or study is a priority and bookshelves or files occupy dominant positions. Comfort is not vital, nor are appearances, but warmth is often keenly sought as air needs fire in order to move. Air does not relate to animals: it is the reasoning process which separates man from them. Arroyo has found that airy people thrive on crisp, dry mountain air.

Fiery people like to live near the hub of things, close to centres of activity. They need open fires, live flames and the sun: a small sun-trap is more important than a large garden – a balcony will do. Sunshine and fire-heat replenish the energy which is the basis of fire vigour. Fiery people are creative or dynamic, and may surround themselves with gadgetry, hi-fi equipment, hobbies' gear or an excess of clothes.

The need for certain elements around us indicates our unconscious search for compatible raw energies. (Did we also notice one we like to avoid?) But it also seems to be true that the qualities of those forces acts as fuel to our spirits, promoting the kind of satisfaction which holds off tiredness. For each of us there is a kind of day that drains our mental resources, and another which leaves us exhilarated rather than tired, even though we have apparently been far busier and ought to be exhausted. This consideration is of great relevance in choosing a career.

A full-time job should satisfy at least two of our prime elements, simply because we spend so much time at it. And at work we need people of similar element bias as colleagues. We complement our natures at home, but at work this is only an

advantage if the jobs themselves are complementary, for instance, dynamic boss and double-checking secretary: even here
one strong element in common will be helpful.

For the earth man or woman, work must entail practical,
tangible usefulness, meeting needs and achieving competence
in areas connected with the five physical senses. Earth confers a
practical touch when combined with another element, for it
'earths' creativity, feeling or abstract concepts and makes them
useful.

Airy people need work which entails structure and criticism,
creating form and order by making a detached or analytical
assessment. Facts must be respected and all steps taken must
be logical. Because thought rules, abstractions may supercede
actual living, and this is how the airy type earns his nickname of
'head-in-air'.

For the fiery-natured, work must entail dynamic or original
experience, rather than useful or logical results. Fire speculates
and dares, either publicly, or privately in visions. Linked with
another element it confers inspiration or ambition but, by itself,
it darts Quixotic, feckless flames.

For the water-conscious, work must involve human contacts,
either physically or in spirit – in the arts, acting or music.
Longings are expressed in sympathetic work, that is, by experiencing the sensitivity of others. Combined with another
conscious element, water lends its sensitivity.

But we do not all work, or even want to. Attitudes to the work
ethic vary, and reasons for choosing to work are numerous. Not
everyone wants to busy his days, and some people find fulfilment in spiritual searching which requires, at least to a certain
extent, withdrawal from living. This withdrawal – if it happens
before retirement age – means cutting short a stage in the
natural cycle of life and, according to some philosophies, a part
of our education. It is generally considered that the natural arc
of human life begins with a mounting, exploring, enlarging
action, followed by a plateau of consolidating achievement
which precedes a final period of assessment and reconciliation.
Arroyo divides this process into four parts, each symbolized by
an element quality:

Schooldays (air) – learning by communication socially and
intellectually;

Apprenticeship (earth) – service with responsibility and deference;

Mastery (fire) – reaping the fruits of personal experience, setting standards;

Inward turning (water) – the education of the spiritual man.

We can appreciate from this that education can stop at any point or can leapfrog, missing out vital stages. According to the functioning of our elements, we are likely to dwell longer in one of these timespans than another. The following suggestions are mine, not Arroyo's.

A hunger for facts and information makes the airy individual a perpetual scholar. He may look for satisfying conclusions, but often continues to make endless connections. He may never move on from this stage.

Earthy fulfilment lies in service and usefulness. Exploratory education may be cut short, mastery never achieved, and self-awareness postponed as long as possible.

Fire seeks to lead and innovate. In learning it is subjective, in achieving self-assertive. Ambition does not hand over to the feeling acceptance of water, for it lives on through its own inspirational intuition. Functioning with earth, fire becomes the steam-roller, powerful, productive – and unstoppable.

Water-consciousness is the wisdom of a feeling response to environment. In old age this is called 'mellowing', but the same response in younger days may involve a withdrawal from the learning of facts, from practical implementation and from activity. It may also result in fervid self-sacrifice to a felt need: vocation is a water concept which 'calls' the individual away from wherever he was and whatever he was doing.

Apart from our work, we allocate our time according to the relative strengths of our element functions. If we do not achieve this in a fair measure – and few of us can spend time just as we would wish – we may become weary, dispirited, demoralized or lethargic. It is therefore wise to split our time into congenial divisions, bearing in mind that, ideally, each element should receive one quarter of our attention.

Without functioning in fire we do not move forward. We have no direction or purpose and are pushed about by the fire of others. Self-assertion need not be destructive: fire only consumes excessively when it takes what is not its own. Without fire functioning, nothing new would ever happen.

Airy occupations include reading, learning facts and theories through the mind, and practising them in written application, mathematics, bureaucracy, computer work or other reasoned pursuits. Logical discussion, systematic mental criticism and the opening of the mind to foreign influences constitute air functioning.

To be fulfilled, the earth function must make use of the five senses positively, with sensual awareness. The body must be respected, cared for, rested and exercised, and its environment attended to, related to and treasured. But as with all element functioning, there is no place for obsession.

The watery function is fulfilled by responding to stimuli with the feelings. Weeping, laughing, enjoying, abhoring, hoping, fearing, sympathizing and getting annoyed are innate parts of us which need to be expressed, not repressed. Darwin tells that most of these responses are common to all mammals. In Greek drama, masks portraying emotions were held before the face so that all might see and apprehend clearly, and so respond themselves. Only when falsely projected through another element do feelings become ugly and dangerous.

The concepts above represent the general principles of the four elements and are vital to their understanding. If one of them is not made explicit in our life, or its functioning is very poor, we are not healthy. The neglected element may cause us a great deal of sorrow, as we shall find presently, and may symbolize an unconscious goal which we cannot hope to reach until we have faced it realistically.

We may grope for it when we have sufficient leisure to stop for a while and allow our unconscious needs to make themselves felt, since the fulfilment of the weakest element is usually concerned with switching off our major driving forces. We turn to this complementary element in order to rest and refresh the parts of ourselves which we use for working. We choose our partners with the same unconscious awareness of need, and this more subtle point will be discussed in the next chapter.

There are those who dislike holidays and are proud to be devoid of hobbies. Such people are either fulfilling all four elements in their everyday lives, which is perfectly possible, or are running from their natural bogeyman – their most neglected or least conscious element. Complementary elements often combine in pairs, so this aspect of element balance may involve a mixture of functions. Nevertheless, there is probably less mystery in the ideas expressed below than in any of the other descriptions of functioning, since these ideas are conscious choices from an early age even though the impulses may not be conscious. Children are far more inclined to rebel against their parents' leisure activities than against following them into a trade or profession.

Depending on other prime elements, the earthy individual on holiday needs adventure, recklessness, romance or intellectual stimulation. He sheds his dullness!

Depending on other dominant functions, the fire-brand sneaks repose, affection, natural surroundings and indolence. He sheds his innovating!

Depending on other elements, the airy person away from work seeks frivolous reading, physical self-indulgence or sport, or foolish, irrational activity. He sheds his reason!

Depending on other dominant functions, water-conscious people look for stimulating activity, exercise, physical pampering, interesting courses or challenges, or serious reading. They shed their feelings!

Only those who live alone or exert their will very strongly can hope to spend all their leisure moments as they like, and the same applies to the way we entertain. We seldom have a completely free hand here, and it is likely to be a matter of compromise: often the members of a partnership, family or group will polarize towards the one fully functioning element they all have in common and will arrange their hospitality in one of the following ways.

Predominant air often uses parties as an escape from the intellect, frequently disappointing guests! Otherwise, discussion must be the focus, and of a very high standard. Introverted air may be gauche and withdrawn and may be found either hiding with a book or trembling beneath the spell of his watery hostess.

The predominantly water-conscious put warm human response first but, whereas extroverted water will want this demonstrated in style, introverted water will draw its guests, probably few in number, inside the personal or family shell. Spiritual water normally seeks solitude and will want around himself only those who respond as he does.

For the earthy, food and comfort predominate. Introverted earth eats well as usual, probably in the kitchen and often in shirtsleeves, with the animals and children. Extroverted earth creates a banquet and makes sure there are seats for all. The same type combined with the fire-function provides an orgy. (Sex is earthy; sexiness is not.)

Visiting introverted fire requires adaptability, for everything depends on the inspiration of the moment. You may find painstaking preparation, but it is equally likely that you will be sent out for fish and chips! The fiery extrovert throws brilliant parties – too dazzling for some – with rather more drink than food.

We must by now have a fairly good idea of our own most conscious and well-fulfilled functions, and we may also, in the course of reading chapter 5, have sneaked a glance at our hands. Their appearance may have suggested propensities which we should never have imagined in ourselves. To this I can only say, take it or leave it. There are vast areas of human wisdom which must remain outside the castles of measurable and traceable truth, though it is to the credit of the exact sciences that the portcullis is lifted the moment their veracity is established. (Humphreys paints a clear picture of the situation when he describes Zen Buddhism as an assault on the citadel of truth.) There is not room in this study to include the gamut of body-language clues which are once more beginning to attract popular attention to the idea that our physical selves express the psyche within. These clues depend chiefly on observation and an awareness of dis-ease. Many of them give early warning of mind/body breakdown yet they remain vagabond, barred from established medical practice through lack of proof.

One modern psycho-physical study which has acquired respect in many countries to the point of receiving university status is graphology. This science, which interprets the marks made in handwriting – itself an electrical impulse from the brain – reveals certain patterns caused by particularly strong and conscious functioning in one element. The ebb and flow of these patterns can be directly related to mood or impulse, so that fluctuations in the writing reflect a shift in mental functioning. The four functions are not always easy to recognize – though they may also be strikingly obvious – but many readers will find the patterns interesting.

Air emphasis concentrates and economizes the writing, aligning it neatly and carefully attending to i-dots and t-bars. Because it takes so many short cuts, airy writing often links i-dots and t-bars to the next letter, and sometimes to the next word. It should not be confused with stylized calligraphic or copybook form, which is an attempt to emulate an admired form and is not a true expression of character. Extroverted air (Sanguineus) will have much larger writing than his introverted counterpart, and it may well have a right slant; but both will make simple, typographic capitals and have clear, unembellished signatures. Air sees life in terms of facts and that includes his conception of himself – which is what a signature portrays. If you find many of these graphological features in your writing, the air function is strongly at work. (Fig. 27)

Most earthy people have a tendency to slow and deliberate, sometimes ponderous, movement, and this propensity is borne out in their handwriting. Earth stabilizes and provides a solid base, and this is evident in the weightiness of pressure and movement. Though the pressure may merely be pasty, opening the nib or flattening the point to produce a woolly trace, the writing is always well planted on the page. (Fig. 29) A heaviness at the base of the letters recalls the lead weighting put into curtain hems to make them hang with dignity. Earthy mental functioning slows the writing but, combined with fiery force, can have the irresistible movement of a steam-roller. This apt term, coined by the American astrologer Dobyns, describes a personality which Jung did not believe to exist but which is quite apparent in the writing of Nelson despite the loss of his right arm.[21]

The qualities of watery people are fluid and receiving, and are shown in their writing by a rounding-out and softening of the letter-forms, giving the script a velvety and uninterrupted flow. Watery patterns are moderately light in pressure, sometimes appearing as garlands and, at other times, as loops. They are not economical movements: they use up plenty of ink; like icing-sugar writing on a cake or toothpaste words on the

Fig. 26   Intuitive fire is overwhelming.

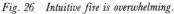

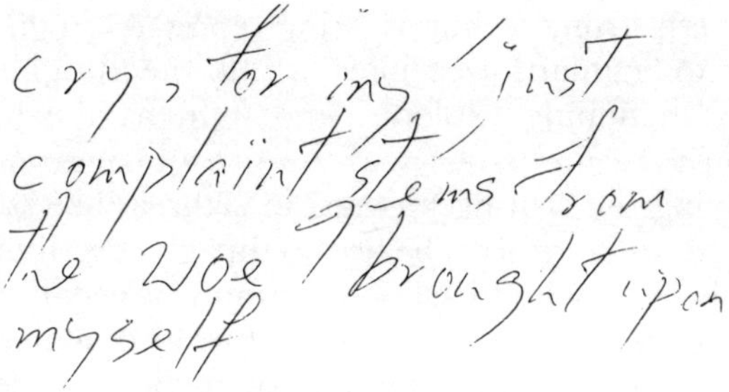

Cry, for my just
complaint stems from
the woe brought upon
myself

Fig. 27   Air predominant, all functions conscious.

Perhaps because manufacturers were prepared to
work long and hard hours themselves (to build
up their businesses), they failed to realise that
their workers had no such incentive. The hard
conditions which employers set for themselves
were intolerable for their employees.

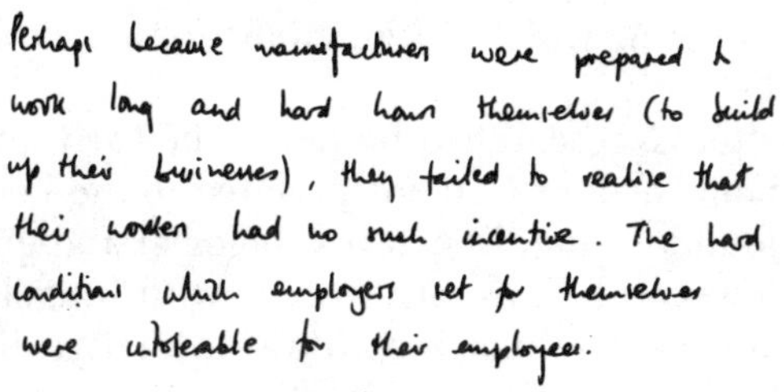

Fig. 28   Water predominant, all functions conscious.

Tonight we'll have some
dinner & then tomorrow
we'll take the plan home.

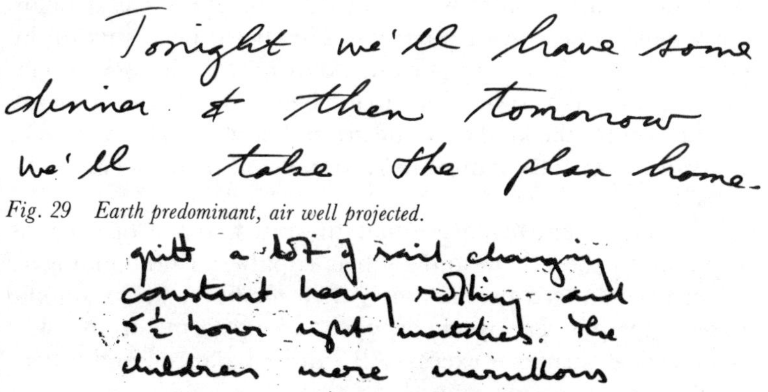

Fig. 29   Earth predominant, air well projected.

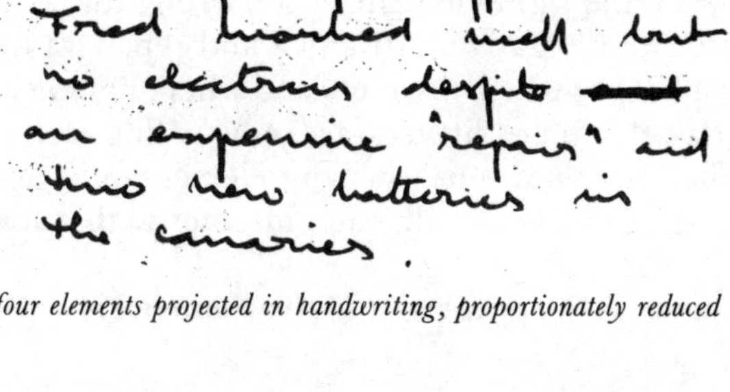

quite a lot of rail changing
constant heavy rolling and
5½ hour night watches. The
children more marvellous
and my self sufficient.
Fred worked well but
no electrics despite
an expensive 'repair' and
two new batteries in
the canaries.

The four elements projected in handwriting, proportionately reduced in size.

bathroom wall, they bend and flow to avoid sharp angles. (Fig. 28) Where strong feeling is being repressed, rogue loops may creep into angular formations, or into the uprights of d and t.

Fire functioning explodes and lightens the handwriting, disconnecting the letters with intuitive inspiration (Fig. 26), but driving the writing forward in a threadlike pattern when hyperactivity prevails. The fire quality gives script rhythm and movement but, where earthy functioning is very lacking, it may also have an unstable appearance. Fire as dynamic force gives the writing energetic impetus, not to be confused with the heavy pressure of earthy endurance. Weakness in fiery expression shows in writing which has no vitality or appears muddy or slow.

These patterns, researched by me in the early stages of my curiosity about the four elements, related to the Four Jungian Functions found by the French psychologist and graphologist Teillard. However, because she worked with Jung, her conclusions are limited and differ in two ways. Firstly, she looks for intuition alone, not dynamic Fire qualities; and, secondly, she will not see intuition/sensation or thinking/feeling as strongly consciously functioning partners. This point brings us to the concluding and most important point of this chapter on element recognition. It has been made before but, because we are about to enter the kind of battle ground described by Milton in *Paradise Lost* (p. 53), it must be re-stated and then held aloft like a banner.

The four elements are equal in status. None of them is superior to the others and each is capable of functioning in superbly balanced productivity, with mediocre or spasmodic expression, in very weak or unconscious form, or in over-balanced, destructive excess. All can be balanced and reconciled.

Each can be the right element in the wrong place. They all have positive and negative, attractive and repellant qualities, but we must be sure which is which, and when. Patience (earth) is not a virtue if you are sitting on a railway line and a train is coming! There are occasions when one element must dominate, and other occasions when all must interact with appropriate balance.

Understanding the properties of the elements is not enough.

Pope's comment that 'Passions, like elements, though born to fight/Yet, mix'd and soften'd, in his work unite,'[22] presupposes a natural conflict between them, and it is one we cannot skirt. It was tackled by the ancients, by Aquinas and by Jung: it is part of the universal character of the physical world and of the human mind, but a great deal can be done about it once confusion or violent antipathy is faced. Gibran saw the conflict in cosmic terms and the whole of *The Prophet*, from which these verses come, contributes to a deeper comprehension.

> Your soul is oftentimes a battlefield, upon which
> your reason and your judgement wage war against
> your passion and your appetite.
> Would that I could be the peacemaker in your
> soul, that I might turn the discord and the rivalry
> of your elements into oneness and melody.
> But how shall I, unless you yourselves be also
> the peacemakers, nay, the lovers of all your elements?
> *The Prophet*, Kahlil Gibran, Heinemann, 1926

The struggle is ultimately a private one, but it will move more quickly towards resolution if we realize how much we reflect and project our inner attitudes on to other people, and upon the world of nature itself. It is easier to look into a mirror than into one's own psyche and, although we may want to deny or discard the image we see there, it is desirable from every viewpoint (analysis, common-sense, feeling response – which may be painful – and productivity) that we now look outwards. We are going to turn away from ourselves towards other people, the people we choose to know or choose to avoid; the people who personify the elements we fear, or the elements we need and strive to possess.

7
The Other Elements

There is every indication that [the] realm of human relationships has taken over that overwhelming load of anxiety and sense of precariousness which had once attached to the natural world. This realm now has a peculiar quality which once characterised the natural world (but apparently does so no longer): a sense of *tight pattern*, of lurking danger and fatality, which at the same time cannot be controlled by rational and intelligible methods.

The Psychoanalytic Movement, Ernest Gellner

Fear of the external elements amounts to a conviction of their hostility and Gellner claims that, despite nature's 'taming' by subjection to intelligible and impersonal laws, those laws are still not fully understood. Many people would maintain that nature is neither tamed nor understood, but that efforts have been made to do both. That is also the most we can say about the internal, mental elements.

Understanding our own most consciously functioning elements is not difficult. The easiest way to confirm the ones we project most clearly is to ask a friend! Our understanding of the other elements is likely to be shaky, prejudiced and therefore darkened a little with fear, though this fear is scarcely ever acknowledged. Looking at our weakest elements – which we must do if they are to be brought into conscious function – involves looking, as Gellner suggests, at other people. We all carry within ourselves the potential to function fully in any element or element combination, but the general inclination of the human mind is to deal with its weakest functions in one of two ways. Either it makes a compensating partner from them through marriage or friendship, or it personifies them in the guise of an enemy. Because the final chapters of this book move towards an appreciation and balancing of all four elements, in which partnerships play a part, we must confront the enemy first and try to come to terms with it.

Jung observed, as we have seen, that the function opposite to the principal function on his compass (p. 106) would probably remain poorly developed and would be badly expressed by the individual. But he also noted that this 'undifferentiated' function tended to project itself on to the person or persons around who most seemed to fit the bill, and this person or 'type' would become an object of intense dislike. Although invested with evil qualities they represented all the unexpressed (because not understood) impulses of the denied nature of the onlooker. In my childhood such a figure was called a *bête noire*: it was considered quite legitimate to have one and no explanation was needed.

Jung believed that this insufferable personage embodied the qualities of the 'opposite' function only. Nevertheless we shall find that our *bête noire* or anti-type often represents a weak combination of elements in ourselves, and is a far more complex figure than Jung depicted; but the attitudes and hatreds caused by negligible functioning in one element make a good starting-point for discussion.

Weakness in air creates a need for visual and physical aids to understanding, such as pictures in books, television rather than newspapers, maps or anything which prevents the need for abstract thought. Centres of learning may be mocked, theories rejected out of hand, discussion considered boring and rules 'kicked at'. The anti-type of those who function poorly in air often pushes out punchy arguments overloaded with polysyllabic words. Worse, he may creep about looking chilly and unapproachable, infinitely wiser-than-thou. His smile is taken as a threat, and real damage may be done to his books if he leaves them lying around. Uniformed officials can be anathema to weak air, and any kind of bureaucrat can invite fury. The bureaucrat or copy-clerk represents air with earth, perhaps the driest of all element combinations since earth and air make dust.

Unconscious or limited functioning in water inhibits the

expression of feeling and may lead to a build-up of emotion. Such people may deride exhibitions of what they call gushing feeling, but are very likely to be trapped by their own. They may be ensnared by false love because they do not know how to experience real love. Unconscious functions are not under control, and it is the individual who functions badly in water who is most prone to irrational outbursts which neither he nor anyone else understands. Many people who think they are emotional (note *think*) are so little concerned with it in general that it remains a weak function and represents for them a difficult area of experience.

Poor functioning in water may project on to the gushing woman (or man) who expresses feelings indiscriminately and leaves no one in any doubt as to the current sentiment. This anti-type may also be given to fondling, kissing with abandon or merely grabbing your elbow. The dreamy water type may also be disliked as 'too deep'.

Negligible functioning in fire often causes inexplicable and ignored hunches, which result in exaggerated scorn of anything cranky or supernatural. There tends to be a similar loathing of 'sniffing into corners' – trying to interpret or find hidden meanings in what has 'a perfectly sensible' explanation. With such an attitude no inspiration or drive is ever consciously projected, though extraordinary things may happen under the influence of drink or physical fear. There may be a deep hatred of those who take risks, boast or conquer.

People whose fire is poorly projected tend to make anti-types of those who put themselves in the limelight or who struggle to change things. They often bitterly resent the success or achievement of others, but accept it in those they do not personally know. The real anti-type is the neighbour 'on the make', whose fire is irritatingly at work before their eyes. Others will find rashness of any kind abhorrent, or may have a particular dislike of self-projection and emotional display, the gushing fountain of the fire-water conscious. (The *fountain* typifies extroverted, fun-loving or 'show-business' behaviour, and can also form an anti-type in the creative artist who seems to be totally motivated by his own feelings and inspiration).

Poor functioning in earth may lead to extraordinary illusions about the body's health,[1] about money and security or any earthy essentials. Unearthed people tend to feel remarkably superior to others: they believe their values are inestimably higher and remain blind to their own failures in service and endurance. They may also be blind to their own greed whilst sneering, Scrooge-like, at the love of material comfort they see around them. The unearthed may have a variety of anti-types, ranging from Doubting Thomas with his lack of faith and imagination to the horsey-doggy type who seems more at home with animals than with human beings. They are not likely to look with favour on the true earth mother who is plain and dowdy (and not at all like her would-be-ethnic middle-class cousin whose house is probably filled with books!). Earthy people may be seen as loathsomely boring and set in their ways, particularly by the fire/earth steam-roller.

This last example shows that a strongly conscious function may find difficulty in reconciliation with another aspect of itself. The fire/earth steam-roller is itself earthy, yet abhors earth. This situation occurs so often that Jung's finding the object of intense dislike solely in an opposing function does not seem consistently valid. I believe that 'blind spots' constantly blur quite well-developed functions and that, within those blind spots, lurk the darkest prejudices, hatreds and fears. They seem to be most often generated when an unconscious element interferes with a conscious one, causing – at the very least – muddle and anxiety.

Most early element concepts held that certain combinations of water, earth, fire and air were incompatible, and Jung detected a similar difficulty between 'opposing' mental functions. The complexity of human character made possible by heredity, conditioning and environment, together with other influences as yet unaccountable, means that any element can make an enemy of another.

This possibility is reflected in nature. Amongst thousands of possible examples here are two which illustrate lack of harmony and the basis of it. The tropical plant which is severely damaged by a northern frost suffers through its own nature, not through the unreasonable (or even unseasonable) nature of the frost. Understanding of the plant's weakness would help avoid its destruction. Dusty topsoil will be washed away by heavy rain, but it is the condition of the soil, and not the rain, which causes the disaster. Before we move on to the essential question of understanding one's own nature, it may be helpful to refer it directly to the natural world in which we have once more found ourselves.

We may instinctively avoid those elements of the greater world whose counterparts we so dislike in mental form. Fear of water, heights, fire or underground caves may spring from poor mental functioning in water, air, fire or earth rather than from a physically traumatic experience: the same may be true of an intense dislike of mud, dust or steam; in that instance a particular combination of two elements is involved. Predominance in one element presupposes weakness or minimal functioning in another, and few of us can avoid being horrified or revolted by at least some aspects of the elements.

Each element represents many aspects of itself, and we may find some aspects tolerable and others not. For instance, the small, brave flame of personal inspiration may be irritating to those who like to go by the rule book at all times, while raging fire (destruction) may sicken those who are considered fiery themselves. We are not even concerned here with positive and negative qualities: these are totally subjective judgements and have no values except as signposts to our own prejudices.

Identifying the anti-type is the first stage in confronting those prejudices and denials of self-fulfilment. Without a good hard look at its behaviour we remain trapped in our confused apprehension. Destructive impulses can arise from uncomprehended impulses, and may cause irrational, even insane or criminal actions. Bryant, a priest, believes all sin to be the outer manifestation of unconscious response: the mugger attacks a defenceless old woman because he will not contemplate the weakness in himself and cannot bear to see it personified. This exaggerated example may be mirrored to a lesser degree in all our lives and, though, we justify our actions at the time, we are actually hitting out blindly to fend off a nameless fear. In middle life we may become filled with dissatisfaction and resentment at our lot, or at our lack of achievement; we may suddenly find ourselves despising our former values because an unconscious attitude is trying to project itself outwards. A Gnostic text suggests in element symbolism the trouble these uncomprehended impulses can cause:

If one does not understand how the fire came to be, he will burn in it, because he does not know his root. If one does not first understand the water, he does not know anything. If one does not understand how the wind that blows came to be, he will run with it. If one does not understand how the body that he wears came to be, he will perish with it. ... Whoever does not understand how he came will not understand how he will go ....[2]

Odious prospects or despised anti-types represent our own blocked energies and, as soon as we face them, they begin to lose their power. Even though we do nothing about them, they are no longer unconscious and inevitably become less destructive. This is a basic tenet of psychotherapy: just as the ancient alchemists sought harmonious rebirth by knowing the origin, so psychoanalysts believe that, by tracing unconscious fears or outdated beliefs to their source, a new approach to life is possible. The Babylonian magi sought to control the malign supernatural influence of demons by addressing that demon by name. Gregory tells how the magician would recite long lists of ghosts and devils to the victim, any one of which might be the cause of his sickness or distress. This prototype word-association test has become extended into the interpretation of dreams and the *transference* of a disturbing behaviour pattern on to the psychotherapist himself. These, with hypnosis and an ever-growing number of psychoanalytical techniques, aim to 'address the demon by name'; to put the finger on the problem.

We may not think we have a problem and, indeed, it is possible to live an unbalanced but fairly happy life, as we shall see. But prejudice and one-sided behaviour also cause problems for our neighbours and, as in the physical world, we may be tempted to think that there are natural laws that make this inevitable. Perhaps we can withold opinion on this point for the time being, while we take a further look at behaviour patterns.

We must now move on from those we could not live with at any price to those with whom we may find ourselves in close contact. We are not talking yet about partners, but about those we see very frequently either from choice or necessity. There will be no more direct mention of blind spots or anti-types but, if we are suddenly aware of an irrational dislike – there they are.

Friendships exist on many levels and unhappiness or discord

can arise through mistaken expectations of the relationship. In his book, *The Four Loves*, C.S. Lewis charts four types of love which in many respects have the nature of the four elements. Sadly, we do not always know which love is functioning between us.

C.S. Lewis's *friendship* is the least natural of the four loves, the least organic or biological. We can live or breed without it. The least jealous of loves, it is critical and selective but remains detached because it chooses to discuss external subjects rather than the friendship itself. Its basis lies in caring about the same truths, and it may encompass many unshared friends. With negative qualities of superiority and pride, this friendship has many of the qualities of air.

Affection is domestic and comfortable, 'decent', full of common-sense with no airs. It is a taken-for-granted love, shared with animals, not expecting much. But it sees any other types of love as nonsense and a threat, and its jealousy may be oddly applied to others' new interests or religious growth, and even to 'things'. This down-to-earth attitude shows in its distrust of the imagination. In its solid practicality it has the qualities of the element earth.

The burning passion of *erotic* love represents to Lewis a complete lack of common-sense (rashness). It is a dangerously consuming passion, creating its own rules – 'Love's Law'. Its negative risk lies in idolatry.

Lewis describes *charity* as a river making its own channel, as magic wine. This love is deep and unselective, loving the unlovable: to Lewis it is the love of God himself, divine love to which man may only hope to attain through God's grace.

These analogies with the elements begin to show us how they behave in friendship, how they tend to react to the behaviour of others.

Watery people like to avoid conflict by letting their feelings flow over or around it,[3] sometimes removing their obstacles – earth, air bubbles and fire – by drenching or by persistent erosion. Their wateriness may become muddy: they may be bogged down, turgid or stagnant if they are also earthy by nature: this particularly placid combination is symbolized in the 'cow by the stream', a *female* aspect which we shall meet again soon. Strongly functioning fire will turn watery feelings into the projected emotion of a turbulent torrent or fountain.

Air-dominant people tend to deal gracefully with conflict, but often harbour enduring resentment because they rationalize their feelings too much at the time. They may argue and try to prove they are right, or become manipulative and persuasive, but more often their dedicated avoidance of the feelings of others will make them noticeable in domestic fracas by their absence. The harmonious combination of air and water produces the 'counsellor', a temperament greatly valued by others but often a torment of indecisive misery to the counsellor himself, as we shall discover.

Fire makes a show of force, swiftly over unless backed up by strong earth. The steam-roller does not give up until its opponent is flattened! Air/fire 'rockets' are easily placated with reason but when fire is mixed with water, there may be fulfilment in conflict or dramatically emotional scenes which leave the 'fountain' happy and everyone else exhausted.

Earthy people absorb the brunt of most difficult situations, since their nature is to endure and accept. But those who live with the earthy know that there comes a point when things quake or erupt – a point to be avoided if possible. Eruptions take the form of an unreasoning outburst of emotion, physical force or a sudden loud lecture, and can gain inexorable momentum if the earthy type summons up fire and turns into the steam-roller.

In the normal course of events we can expect dominant elements to be characterized by a general pattern of behaviour. We can, for instance, usually expect watery people to be subjective, since feeling embraces what is cherished and rejects whatever is disliked. Extroverted water values its place in society and enjoys being liked. Its standing is of prime importance. Introverted water may have a calm manner, since feelings penetrate inwards here, but, unless the feeling is spiritual, the water may be bottled up as unexpressed emotion, detrimental to health. The judgement of the water-dominant is not always taken seriously since it is so subjective – in spite of Jung's insistence that the feeling is a rational one[4] – but we are all grateful for the understanding, sympathy and sharing of our 'watery' friends.

Others' reactions to us are largely governed by our own

dominant elements, and are best described in terms of the natural elements. A need to be contained draws water to earth, but it distrusts the unconsidered flare of fire and tries to deflect it, often making it spit or splutter, and occasionally dousing it. Water is fascinated by air's capacity for detachment and sometimes reflects its views for a while, but generally shuns in the end its remoteness and lack of feeling. It becomes obvious how so many marriages between water and air inevitably occur (viz. Arthur Miller – Marilyn Monroe), and, equally inevitably, founder.

The predominantly earthy person is unsurpassed in realism: French psychologists call the sensation function the 'fonction du réel.'[5] Jung described the life of this type as 'an accumulation of actual experiences with concrete objects'.[6] Extroverted earth may be a crude pleasure-seeker, taking enormous care of himself and his sensual desires, but he may also be a painstaking handyman or business man – the sort who follows the company line with total loyalty. He may be an expert craftsman or surgeon, an engineer or a nurse. Introverted earth may appear calm, but his inability to understand his experiences, which he draws inwards and downwards rather than discarding or translating them into practical use, makes it impossible for him ever to account for his behaviour.[7] (Introverted earth is the least likely reader of this book.)

Earth needs water to be fertile, and is refreshed and softened by it. Earthy types can absorb watery feelings up to a point without effort but, if bogged down by them, become truly melancholic. Earth needs relatively little fire or it becomes scorched and ceases to be productive – though it can quench it with heavy sods of reality – and, whilst it can cooperate with air it does not like to be blown about by it, nor is it willing to rise with it. Its greatest partnership with air is embodied in the bureaucratic or copy-clerk who observes and classifies, putting facts to work.

The predominantly airy person may present either of two very different images, but detached preoccupation with concepts and theories can turn the utterances of both into a string of facts, or analysis for analysing's sake. Either may seem curiously devoid of passion or interest in social life; both may be lacking in religious fervour, physical care or artistic discrimination. But, whereas the extrovert is a smooth politician, 'airing' his opinions and persuading with apt phrases, introverted air can appear gauche and unworldly, immature in all but his chosen sphere of study.

Air finds water irritatingly fluid, but may be unconsciously drawn to it and, as has already been suggested, it is quite common for the airy type to be swept off his feet by the flow. This happens to both sexes. When air burns with fire it achieves and creates new knowledge, but it is the fire which is using air, and not the other way round, and a fiery nature is needed to fire the rocket! Without fire, air tends to circulate rather than move on. Airy-fairy argues fruitlessly with earth-man, each telling the other to heed the 'facts' while one propounds theory and the other obeys sense-perception. Generally, air allows earth to be his servant, a firm rock above which he can freely wander in the abstract.

If you have a ball of fire around you, you will be used to sparks of unrepressed and forward-looking optimism. The fiery person tends to use others or ignore them, and his zeal inspires envy or exasperation since he has no respect for the convictions of others. His loyalty is always to the possibilities of the moment and, when these vanish, so does he. His activities may alter with capricious speed, leaving onlookers confused and breathless, and he will learn new skills fast while he is still inflamed by their possibilities. But introverted fire inspires a visionary cut off from reality, an enigma to his neighbours, forbidding his mind to embrace uncongenial prospects.[8] His may be the voice crying in the wilderness, for introverted fire contains the flame of prophecy. Because fire is self-centred, dynamic and urgent, it has a bad reputation for friendship and, in particular, for sexual or romantic fidelity. It is likely to use (and use up) what the other elements have to offer, snatching research from the air type, service and faithfulness from the earthy, and feeling – if it can – from the watery.

How, we may well wonder, are partnerships, close and enduring relationships, ever formed, let alone maintained, with all this unfortunate interaction?

From an early age we admire attributes we do not possess. We try to harness them for our own benefit, joy, comfort or stimulation, in truth, to make up for our own deficiencies.

Later, the mutual choosing of life partners is an extension of that habitual need. We may realize rather late that negative or misunderstood elements come with the deal, and may prevent, by their relentless grip on our unconscious, a fulfilment of what had seemed to be a perfect blending.

We hope to find our strengths appreciated and our weaknesses complemented, but can this ever happen? A partner who embodies only our own poorest functions will be a strange bedfellow, a creature from another realm of living whom we can never hope to understand well. Jung describes this as falling in love with our projected *animus* or *anima*, the seed of the opposite sex within ourselves (as shown in the T'ai Chi symbol) and an unconscious psychological force. The attraction of a sexual opposite may not be as great as the attraction of the qualities which we lack.

We must pause briefly here to consider, but by no means to exhaust, the question of a natural division between the male and the female. It has been suggested many times in this book that the division of the Absolute or One into two aspects (itself a fall from perfection) brought about a concept of masculine and feminine opposites. Beginning with the marriage of Sun and Moon, and progressing to Sky Father and Earth Mother, most ancient religious concepts found a male-female balance throughout nature. The male represented active, *Apollonian* functions (fire and air), and the female the yielding *Dionysiac* stance (earth and water).[9] Medieval understanding of this contrast is shown in the Dauphin's appreciation of his horse! 'He is pure air and fire; and the dull elements of earth and water never appear in him but only in patient stillness while his rider mounts him.'[10]

In this study air and fire in combination produce the rocket, and the cow by the stream represents the qualities of water and earth. But as with the Dauphin's horse, both are most truly blended within one entity. It is known that the human body contains both male and female potentiality, and the human psyche also has both dimensions: were this not so, men and women would not understand one another at all. As it is, the Dionysiac elements can predominate in a man's mentality, and the Apollonian in a woman's. For the rest of our consideration of intereacting elements we must forget about men and women and remember only that, in partnerships, one aspect may very often represent our nature and the other our fulfilment. The *Natural Psychology* of Anelog provides a unique, speculative understanding of this situation.[11]

Fortunately we are usually drawn to a partner who has one major element in common with one of our own dominant functions, as well as one which represents a weak or difficult area in ourselves. At times of great estrangement the mutual element can be the means of reconciliation, a restorer of faith in the partnership and a pathway into a shared future.

As a strong, shared element, water pulls the partners into a deep, private pool of feeling, where conversation is not always needed since understanding is on a profoundly caring level of gentleness.

The earthy person needs an earthy partner, because the earthbound attitude can be just too exasperatingly restrictive for many! As a strong, shared element, it establishes a stable, practical working life. Earthy couples are often puzzled by the extraordinarily 'senseless' motivations of others who have different ideals or who waste money on partnership break-ups.

As a shared element, air makes for a calm, even cold life, with endless futile rationalizing of the other elements and little warm (or violent) expression.

Combined fire may provide a cabaret for the neighbours with its spectacular rows and frequent changes in routine. But this plate-throwing partnership is intensely satisfying to the fiery type: it thrives on outbursts of self-projection and is often – despite appearances – devoted and enduring.

Most partnerships involve a sexual relationship and this is characterized by our most dominant elements. The silent or murmuring devotion of combined water may contrast markedly with the constant verbal checking of airy couples, whose love-making is not satisfying unless it is explained and justified at all stages. Earth simply gets down to it in animal fashion, concentrating on the sexual act itself and not easily deterred by objectionable surroundings or outside interruptions. Combined fire suffers from boredom and will do much to introduce sparks of innovation; it contrives to bring in a quality of the unexpected and is easily rendered unfaithful by routine performance.

Who is to judge a perfect partnership, and on what grounds? Does the harmony of a *folie à deux* – which may be totally concentrated in one or two elements – equal the full-blooded scenario of a marriage where the rocket, the fountain, the counsellor, the steam-roller, the copy-clerk and the cow by the stream live under one roof in a fifty-year drama? And is it perhaps not easiest for the chaos of the elements to find order in a partnership of two people of one sex?

These are questions which bring into focus the matter of ultimate balance, the quintessence produced by complete blending, and we shall not be following up the wisdom of ancient minds on that subject here. But the task of counterpoise, of generating a harmonious balance between four seemingly opposed forces in order to sustain a partnership, is one which is very much the business of this moment. For a short while we will turn from intimate relationships and lift our eyes to a wider perspective.

Natural, complementary forces balance one another in all aspects of life, and function at their best when attempting equilibrium. Sadly, each aspect tends to think it is complete and seldom values its natural partner:

	Masculinity	**Femininity**	
Fire	Technology	Fertility	Water
with	Scientific	Ecology	with
Air	discovery and		Earth
'The rocket'	invention	Family life	*'The Cow*
	Theories	Stability	*by the*
	Progress	Status quo	*stream'*

	Left brain	**Right brain**	
Air	Proven facts	Intuitive	Fire
with		inspiration &	with
Earth	Rules and codes	creativity	Water
	Law enforcement	Religious	
'The copy		experience	*'The fountain'*
clerk'	Curricula	Spontaneity	
		Leisure impulses	

	Self-assertion	**Self-denial**	
Earth	Material prosperity	Liberalism	Water
with	and achievement	Philanthropy	with
Fire	Physical survival	Committee work	Air
'The steam-roller'	Ambition	Psychotherapy	*'The counsellor'*
	Competition	Diplomacy	
	Brutality		

The hi-tech aspect of science, the Apollonian function of active research, has been depicted as a rocket which zooms off into the future with total disregard for feeling or ecology. If technology interferes with the balanced interchange of natural resources beyond a certain point, our ecosystem will become more than polluted – it will be consumed. There is no more wilderness to develop. On the other hand, men and animals do not always survive for very long if left to their own ecosystem. There is evidence of disease and early mortality amongst pre-technological peoples, and Keith Thomas tells us that the average life-span of man a mere three centuries ago was 29.6 years. It would not take the most dedicated drop-out long to think of a modern technological invention for which he is grateful. The rocket and the cow by the stream are both right and they can both be wrong.

Whilst fire-air makes intuitive but fact-based leaps forward, earth-air tests them and establishes rules, systems and codes. It does not permit any kind of irrational or inspirational belief to interfere with what has already been proved. Earth and air make dust, in which nothing can grow and in which everything is, in a sense, dead or of the past. (It also symbolizes the world of established law and order, the unbending system of restraints which can be at times bizarrely inapplicable, making the law an ass.)

Earth-air is balanced by the fountain, symbol of fire with water and embodiment of two kinds of intuition. In modern terms, the copy-clerk signifies left-brain activity which concerns itself with rational and tangible processes, while the fountain represents the right-brain faculty for intuitive understanding. The very fact that our brains have made provision for both functions should suggest a need for their balance. The fountain symbolizes all that is inspirational – the hunches, nameless desires, visions, impulses and convictions of our irrational 'truth'.[12] It also represents leisure, freedom to follow our whims and do as we feel like doing, unrestricted by our own habitual rule-book. The fountain has an important role, but put in sole charge it mounts uncontrollably, soaking and engulfing all the forces of reason. Jung warned that paying too much attention to the underworld of irrational experience can put fantasy in control, that the conscious mind must supervise or balance intuitive exploration. Supervision means overlooking, not ruling: thus we are talking of implementation, not tyranny, on the part of the copy-clerk.

Our last symbolic partnership has a long history of conflict. The steam-roller can represent material prosperity and achievement, the ruthless propulsion of practical purpose towards specific ends. Vividly symbolized by the industrial revolution, it remains to a large extent the ideal set before the young, who are exposed from birth to the promise of buy-and-you-will-be. Implicitly, material success brings every other kind of success in its train, including sexual attraction and power – the clout said to be acquired through a high standard of living. The steam-roller also signifies survival, since strong fire-earth qualities confer immense stamina. The steam-roller drives inexorably towards a self-inspired end, and it may be charged with ambition, competition or brutality.

The aims of survival exclude sensitivity, caring and reflection, and the counsellor is by nature thoughtful and caring. (If this conflict seems familiar it is because it centres on the *self-denial* aspect of Western religious teaching.) Yet, remembering Jung's belief that feeling and thinking could not function together, a certain degree of conscious cooperation is needed if the counsellor is not to vacillate between two conflicting attitudes of mind. He must be made aware of his gifted and valuable role, which is the closest to 'fair judgement' to which man can aspire. It applies both moral reasoning and empathy to any situation, and is not often moved to hasty action.

Yet the counsellor's role is often a source of frustration to himself. Anthony Storr warns that he cannot be a leader, teacher or solver of problems, and may feel himself to be a 'non-person'. Clearly, he requires the vigorous balance of the steam-roller function. The compromise needed between these two combinations is the stuff of which committees are made, the steam-roller's brakes being held by the counsellor and the counsellor slowly moving towards a course of action.

I believe mankind often seeks a balance without being aware of it: like a dog eating grass we grope instinctively for an antidote to our ills. Descartes was a profoundly religious man whose naturally airy imbalance made him account for his beliefs, but his religious impulses were probably not rational. We find it very satisfactory when gifted or well-known role-players extend their vision to new horizons or show eccentric preoccupation with fields other than their own, because we see in this an attempt to become whole. The nineteenth-century American psychologist William James was aware of the need to investigate what we could call the other side of our coin of consciousness, when he wrote: 'No account of the universe in its totality can be final which leaves these other forms of the consciousness quite disregarded.'

Partnership with others involves appreciation of qualities which are not our own most obvious functions of expressions. It also involves respect for criteria not our own. The scientist Crick deplores philosophy's lack of understanding of the language of information processing (see Chapter Notes. Introduction, 3): the philosopher Koyré believes in turn that most of the difficulties of contemporary science proceed from a neglect of a metaphysical foundation! These comments are probably true but they are pointless: one might as well say that a man is faulty in being unable to bear a child.[13] It is not a part of his function to do so and, if he wants a child he must cooperate, not change his nature. Feet and hands do not do the same work, and no one wastes time saying that they should. But when they work together in a state of mutual respect rather than mutual distrust, the resulting harmony can surpass the powers of either of them.

8
Towards a Balance

The fire, the water, earth, and air, we know,
All in one plant agree to make it grow.
Must man, the chiefest work of art divine,
Be doom'd in endless discord to repine?
No, we should injure Heaven by that surmise,
Omnipotence is just, were man but wise.
The Beaux-Stratagem, Act III, Sc.iii. George Farquhar

Farquhar saw his Restoration comedy as no more than 'a well-framed tale handsomely told as an agreeable vehicle for counsel and reproof', and would not have supposed that his wit would pose fundamental and unanswerable questions. Much of the surmise above is unacceptable to scientists of any discipline – biology, physics, chemistry, genetics or psychology. They would dismiss it – including the final reproof – though they would say they were questioning the creative process rather than a divinity. Few of those who have studied human response in any depth would suggest that people are born with equal or necessarily harmonious attitudes to life.

The idea of a divine soul at the centre of all created matter can only be held as a matter of intuitive faith. This does not mean it is untrue, simply that it has not yet been proved by man and categorized as a fact. Empirical science has, instead, spent 500 years reducing man's nature to accountability, a process spearheaded by Copernicus, Darwin and Freud. Gellner says that the first of these 'removed man from the centre of the universe, the second assigned man back to nature and among the other animals, and the third showed man that he was not even master in his own house'.

What, then, is man supposed to have in his mind at birth? It is necessary to understand a little of the scientific viewpoint. Darwin found many human attitudes to be 'instinctive' – innate reactions inherited through the genetic chain. He found that individual babies and young animals showed widely differing capacities for feeling, initiative and intelligence,[1] and these owed nothing to environment. The socio-biologist Barash has speculated further that 'we have no gene for walking, but our genetic make-up ensures that we develop the anatomy that will make walking possible, in fact unavoidable. Is there a certain mental anatomy that makes certain customs likely to develop?' Alister Hardy believes that a function of the brain exists in both man and animals which acknowledges a higher power; that religion may be an inherited organic sense.

Rose complains that the claims of genetics have now encroached to the point where biological necessity would appear to justify racial differences and 'all society's unfair social arrangements', together with schizophrenia, homosexuality and a host of other issues once considered to be moral questions. These claims have also reached the point where some scientists are turning, despite the establishment of a genetic DNA code in the 1950s, to the type of thinking pioneered by Abraham Maslow (d. 1970). Maslow refused to see human beings as animals or as victims of their physiological needs: he believed that many aspects of human nature could not be accounted for in that way and were higher and specifically human functions. His work resulted in a humanistic psychology whose main object was spiritual growth.

Other twentieth-century scientists have insisted that our behaviour patterns are conditioned by circumstances following birth, and that we have to learn to free ourselves from these partly conscious, superimposed restraints. A recent book in which a biologist, a geneticist and a psychologist collaborated, suggests that 'interactionism is the beginning of wisdom', that inherited tendencies, conditioning and environment can combine to form character, and that no one can predict what perception of the world this will bring about.[2] That perception *is* man in his uniqueness, not only in his behaviour but in the impulses upon which he does not act and in the unconscious reactions which he does not even know he is experiencing. His perception is further taken, by those who are discovering increasing links between the mind and the physical state of the body, to influence his health; to send messages into the very cells of the body telling them whether to live or die, suffer or embrace life.[3]

Our perceptions are both absolutely real and absolutely dispensable. Nature may have given us certain predispositions, but nature does not dictate what we do. She gives us many warnings, demonstrating through her handiwork the likely outcome of slavish obedience to a predisposition. We shall return to this, the final issue of the study, very shortly.

Science may be undecided about the sources of our perception and its precise character at birth, but other patterns of thinking claim to understand how and why we should react specifically to set stimuli. Several creeds teach that the soul, an etheric spirit without tangible form, returns to inhabit human form many times and that the task of self (soul) knowledge is renewed by its rebirth in another body. The soul is reborn in the same state as it left its last life, its elements evolved to that point only and awaiting new opportunities for growth. Such creeds expect a lack of balance at birth, but they also anticipate self-examination and change.

Some Christians believe that the soul carries within it the marks of 'original sin', the misused free will of Adam. This has also been interpreted as Jung's *shadow*. Bryant claims that, 'The sin which dwells in a person is precisely what Jung personifies as the shadow. It acts like a sub-personality gathering to itself despised and rejected elements . . . .'

The schools of astrology and other so-called esoteric arts hold that a complex pattern of cosmic influences triggers responses at birth in the brains of babies which carry a genetic propensity for those particular qualities. These planetary influences have been neither proved nor disproved, though attempts are being made which hope to meet the criteria of scientific certainty.[4] But even if it is proved that we are by nature unbalanced or given to excessive functioning in one element, it does not mean we have to live through a set pattern of inevitable events or become an archetypal witness to its qualities. The opportunities for growth are greatest when we understand the composition of our raw material.

It may be that we seem to have been endowed by nature in one particular aspect and that, through it, our perception leads to remarkable success. We cannot always be sure of the influences which make us function so well in this one aspect but, when our entire bent is towards it, we must take care that we are not also moved towards our own destruction. Biased perception may give birth to its own religion. A nature which is dominated by air, the thinking process, tends to exclude from its own reality all that does not serve the divinity of reason. Such a religion is Marxism but, on a lesser scale, many academics cannot perceive the world in conscious terms unless it explains itself with footnotes. The gourmand, the sport-obsessed and the over-materialistic are in danger of worshipping earth, the tangible element.

Excessive water drowns and those who allow their feelings to control them may eventually, like Ophelia – 'a creature native and indu'd/Unto that element' – submit to a current which carries them away from earth, reason and action.[5]

Nature seems set at times on teaching hard lessons by making examples of those who do not weigh and balance their perceptions, who throw in their lot with one attitude, one element alone. She warns that fierce, uncontrolled fire can consume and destroy the other elements. The whizz-kid, forever on the move, despising those who dream or 'get stuck in a rut', becomes a living fire-brand. Unless he stops to consider, reflect and consolidate he may explode or burn himself out. The justice of omnipotence shows itself in the tragic failure of those who allow themselves narrowly restricted perception; such people formed the basis of Jung's research for *Psychological Types*.

Teillard reminds us that 'a large portion of the psychological troubles from which this world suffers comes from the unequal development of these four functions, which are the means of adapting to the world'. People who were over-developed in one function, their feeling or their thinking, for instance, colouring their entire personalities like letters through a stick of rock, filled the case-books of Jung, Freud and Adler, and today fill mental hospitals and agencies for the inadequate.

Unfortunately, they also fill seats in high places. Too often their fanaticism is not noticed until their god is being generally worshipped, and too often this humiliating experience causes their ex-followers to put another, opposing god in its place in compensation. This is the cycle of politics, each faction claiming that its manifesto is 'reasonable', this still being the password of our civilization.

It happens, too, in private lives. We hear of – we may be – the kind of people who spend our adult lives doing the things we were forbidden as children, and avoiding the gods which had preoccupied our parents. Conversely, we may grow up admiring falsely the qualities – elements – we were taught to admire, and tempted always to claim them for ourselves. This way of looking at things produces in the end a severely inhibiting Super-Ego; a system of superimposed behavioural instructions beneath which the self squirms and pleads. Our perceptions are as often muddled or darkened as they are overbalanced, and as much inhibited as they are exaggerated.

This instant in time is probably burdened with oudated perceptions. The way our parents influenced our youth is history which we need to know in order to be able to observe it, not to carry it around like a disability certificate. Do we let it, for instance, stop us trusting our own inspirations or urges to action? If we do, we are quenching our fire function. Do we let it affect our opinion of learning or of our own capacity to learn? If we do, we are stifling our air function. Do we let it prevent us from daring to show our feelings, or from approaching others with open compassion or dislike? If we do, we are wasting our water function and probably creating much suffering for ourselves. Do we let it excuse our lack of practicality, our inability to look after our physical needs or our frigid refusal to enjoy our bodies? If we do, we are denying the earth function.

Brave individuals are able to transcend the most crippling genetic disadvantages when they refuse to accept that they are disadvantaged. They confront not their handicaps but the world itself, seeing it as available for them, too. Their attitude is fundamental and brings us right into the centre of the four-element concept and the gifts of sanity and reality it has to offer us.

The human condition has not changed. Our survival as a species is due less to conquering than to adapting, to recognizing and accepting the way of things.[6] If we are cleverer than our ancestors it is because we have studied ourselves and our environment and applied our knowledge with skill; if we are less happy than they were it is because we allow our learning to blind us to certain unchanging realities around and within us. This applies both to the natural world and to its reflection in the mind.

We are an intrinsic part of this earth. Our bodies are born of, and grow by means of, surrounding material; it is our birthright to display and add to the beauty of that matter as fishes and birds enhance their own environments. All natural processes affect us and we ignore them to our cost. Learning seldom helps us to draw closer to the natural world; why is it that the loss of a faculty so often seems to bring the cosmos into vivid new perspective? Man no longer has any excuse either to abuse or distrust the external elements, and his future happiness must depend on a more sensible (using all the senses) coexistence with them, beginning with the response of each individual. I believe that the Druids – and later Wordsworth – did sense a particular quality of nature in places where the air, water, sunlight and earth met in equal and intense projection – a quintessence not to be derided until it has been well experienced. Its therapeutic effect may one day be acknowledged by those who seek to interfere with nature's processes. It is the magic sought by alchemists and the peasant's rapport noted by Jung: 'When you walk with naked feet, how can you forget the earth?'[7] The living power of nature is still there for man to absorb and repay, but we express it only to the extent of our conscious use of it.

Nature teaches us many lessons which we know but choose to forget. As the four seasons give meaning to man's lifespan, his maturing, fruition, autumnal inner growth (and in some creeds his dying before re-birth), so floods, droughts, earthquakes and conflagrations teach us that, if we overuse one element and neglect another, our whole being will reflect a lack of equilibrium. Heraclitus understood that each time one of the elements consumed another, their natural balance was rearranged: 'Fire lives the death of air, and air lives the death of fire; water lives the death of earth, and earth that of water.'[8]

On a practical level, this can happen in the course of our daily routine. If we consider our waking day as a stretch of sixteen hours, four should, ideally, be given to each element – each 'season'. There will be overlapping of interests; there may even come a joyful moment when all four seem to reach their peak together, but this quintessence, Eliot's 'moment of intersection of the timeless with the time', is the subject for another book. For most people it is a step forward simply to resolve not to spend more than four hours of any one day in the same element, and to try to nurture them all. (We noted earlier that a job of work should fulfil two markedly conscious elements.)

This deliberate effort at balance has been the most enriching idea I have yet discovered. It is not a religion: it is just a helpful concept, and a very old one. Air involves the orderly application of the mind. Fire produces a movement towards the future and fans sparks of creativity. Earth consolidates the physical situation and surroundings. Water 'floats down a stream between two banks of reality' (Tagore), helped by love, music and beauty in all their forms.

The balance within the mind requires acceptance, action, thought and feeling awareness: four elements; four attitudes. We can enter a state of conscious cooperation with the least compatible of the elements by understanding the way in which it appears to begin to function within us. Philosophers before and since Plato have assigned different parts of the body to the centering of various psychic experiences, and the development of techniques to harness this natural energy was perhaps brought to its greatest extension by Gurdjieff in the first half of this century.[9] Steiner, a German-born theosophist who died in 1925, developed his own system which attempted to explain the world through the nature of man. The precise relationship between the physical matter of man's body and the cosmos which surrounds him is not known; undoubtedly, there is a relationship and it may hold the secrets of healing towards which some aspects of modern medicine are groping. The following centres are real to me, and the centre any reader perceives for himself is equally valid. The important thing is that all four should be in positive working order.

Thinking develops from a willingness to learn and equate facts, and is centred in the head. But first, the mind must be swept clear of misconceptions: winds of change must blow away the fogs and mists of prejudice because facts are learned one at a time and in sequence, and can only be linked correctly when visibility is clear. Those who think they cannot learn need, first, a change of air and then the knowledge that they must ask for the facts one at a time and in the correct order. If they cannot find a teacher who will instruct them in this way, then they are right and the teacher is wrong. The energy patterns of air are rational (in ratio) and can be learned:[10] those of the other elements must, traditionally, be assimilated without conscious effort.

Fire is a forward leap of the spirit and is traditionally experienced in the breast.[11] When early man first handled physical fire he undoubtedly fled from his unwitting creativity and abandoned its consuming force; eventually, he realized that it was his fire and that he could use it as he liked. The first little flame, the re-kindling of an impulse to action, represents the taking of light from under a bushel and offering it to the world. When the heart leaps with eager intention a fire is lighted. That is the beginning.

Feeling comes from low down, within the bowels or the guts.[12] It uses the body's stillness, and the body must be still to receive this profound awareness. The monk who asked where he could find the entrance to the path of truth was told to listen to the murmuring of the brook,[13] and there is an affinity between feeling response and the actual presence of water. Water has gifts of revelation and release, and sitting beside it or bathing within it may be the start of a better relationship with the feeling function. The deep warm bath – the return to the womb so needed by many of us for relaxation of the spirit – is a direct invitation to the feeling function, and is the more therapeutic for being consciously acknowledged.

Earth is applied strength and endurance, concentrated through the senses. As a relatively poorly earthed person I receive this force most powerfully through the feet. Acceptance, earthiness, is learned through simple living and an awareness of the pattern of nature in her seasons. Farmers, however mechanized their farms, watch with respect the movements of nature and do not pit themselves against her. Tilling the soil and caring for animals was once thought the right cure for mental distress since it moves the centre of consciousness from the head to the body.

'As above, so below'. The Hermetic message of cosmic unity throughout all creation was that nature's laws are universal.[14] As in the macrocosm, if fire is used in excess the body is consumed, burnt out. When watery feeling surges unchecked, the whole self is flooded and made impotent. If the earthy senses take complete control of the mind, feeling and spirit are numbed into a less-than animal condition of torpor, but if thought dominates, the body and all its impressions below the neck become an arid wasteland without expression or beauty of their own.

In contemporary terms, we experience positive or negative feedback from the natural elements: this is something which can be improved upon simply by recognition of the existence of a holistic pattern. We may feel differently, think differently, respond more sensitively and behave differently in consequence, and that is the beginning of equipoise. It is no new cult, but man's most ancient wisdom, built into his natural programming and capable of adaptation to environment.

Whereas Farquhar's plant could only hope to fulfil a limited master plan, the faculty of conscious awareness enables us to acknowledge what seems to be our most natural propensities and then mark out and supervise our own growth patterns, using even those energies we considered least within our grasp. We may not be able to change our nature but we can alter our responses. Nobody ever said the world was fair: it is full of unbalanced attitudes, just as its natural resources seem to distribute themselves without justice; but each human being has the capacity for growth through conscious awareness. If he chooses to live amidst a chaos of the elements, that is his pleasure. If he turns to polarized aspects of living because he fails to contemplate the relative strengths and weaknesses within himself, that is his choice. But if he listens with his body as well as his mind to the shifting arrangements of the elements around him, he may come to an understanding not of, but with, the world.

Appendix A Brain and Mind

We must differentiate at once between the human *brain*, which is a physical organ, a machine capable of precise scientific testing, and the *mind*, which represents the activity of the brain as a whole and is the product of the interaction of cellular processes – the *result* of brain events. Unskilled laymen, myself included, can hypothesize on *mind* functioning, but only those biologists with access to refined equipment can assess *brain* processes.

Any authoritative work on brain evolution begins with words which amount to, 'very little is known positively about this'. Investigations of animal brains show an advance amongst reptiles over fish and amphibians. They have an extra layer of nerve tissue which denotes the beginnings of the cerebral cortex – later to develop in man to such an extent that multiple folding or convolutions became necessary. Biologists since Darwin have emphasized that nature did not design the brain but that it came as a result of evolutionary accidents which happened to produce helpful features – both mental and physical – that at each stage gave an advantage to organisms possessing them.[1] When a feature became redundant, however, it did not necessarily disappear, even though as an innate response it was no longer particularly helpful. No one knows exactly where or how memories are stored but scientists who have studied 'redundant helpful responses' believe them to lie in the *old* or *reptilian* brain, the most anciently evolved part of the forebrain.[2] E.O. Wilson thinks they are responsible for tribalism and territorial claiming, Sagan believes them to function in the ritual actions of children, in dreams and in some psychotic illnesses, and Maclean regards them as predominating in such states as epilepsy and nymphomania. The old brain eludes intellectual tactics because its primitive, animal structure makes it impossible to communicate in verbal terms.[3] Any human being of sane mind should expect it to play a small part in his behaviour, with his environment, conditioning and conscious will gradually, but never entirely, eradicating its archaic processes.[4] Thus, for example, does a timid man leap into violent attack if his wife or children are threatened.

Innate responses are not the same as intuitive ones though, before the *right brain* was located and named, unreasoned discoveries were attributed to animal instinct. Intuition is a cognitive ability, housed with the rational/verbal function within the (cerebral) neo-cortex.[5] This was discovered through the study of brain-damaged individuals. Accidents or strokes in the left hemisphere can impair the ability to read, write, speak and do arithmetic; similar lesions in the right hemisphere can impair three-dimensional vision, pattern and facial recognition, musical ability and holistic reasoning, and the power to conceive poetry but not to rhyme it. In a highly reasoned, intellectual society, the right brain tends to be undervalued although its functions are of vital and practical importance and without them Sagan considers intellectual progress to be 'sterile and doomed'.

The findings of socio-biologists during this century, and especially since the defining of the DNA genetic code in the 1950s, are subject to constant revision.[6]

Jung created the term *archetype* to describe the primordial images which recur in the psyche of man and which may have formed themselves during the thousands of years when the human brain and consciousness were emerging from an animal state.[7] These images of fear had been noted by Charles Lamb in *Essays of Elia*.

'Gorgons, and Hydras, and Chimeras dire-stories of Celaeno and the Harpies – may reproduce themselves in the brain of superstition – but they were there before. They are transcripts, types – the archetypes are in us, and eternal.'

Darwin later agreed with the theories of psychological evolution put forward by Herbert Spencer, believing that 'the necessary acquirement of each mental power by gradation' did not banish primeval beliefs. Some of these unconscious images were expressed in the inexplicable terrors of childhood: such paralysing horrors as bogeymen, darkness, faces at the window, skeletons, ghosts or repulsive creatures were related to man's earliest experiences and carried, genetically and intact, in the human brain. Sagan adds to this the notion that, like gill-slits in the foetus, primeval fears disappear naturally when they are found to be inappropriate or unnecessary.

Appendix B The Chinese Elements

The Tao, which is translated as the 'Way', but is actually two signs for head and way, was an ethnic religion centuries before Confucianism or Buddhism became merged with it, and has a legendary history of well over 4000 years. Central to its philosophy is the concept of polarities (Palmer prefers 'tensions') between the Yin and the Yang in nature. The four elements of fire, water, air and earth are the basis of the world creation.

The original Great Yang and Great Yin were the sun and moon: the sky was father and the earth was mother. Yin qualities are shown in the traditional diagram below as a short line, while Yang qualities have a longer line.

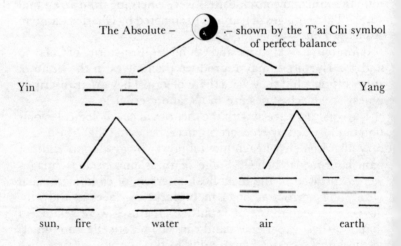

The Absolute – shown by the T'ai Chi symbol of perfect balance

Yin   Yang

sun, fire   water   air   earth

It will be seen that no element is entirely Yin or Yang, though each has a predisposition towards one or the other. Their source within the T'ai Chi – itself containing a natural balance of polarities – prevents the elements from being wholly Yin or Yang. Their dynamic force, equated by Capra with forces operating in modern physics, produces harmonious effects throughout physical existence. *Feng-shui*, the balance between wind and water vital to healthy house-siting, is mentioned in chapter 4 but, for a perfect image of dynamic and harmonious elemental interaction, read Wilhelm's translation of *The Secret of the Golden Flower* (mentioned in Jung's *Psychology and the East*.) This image is also the basis of Eliot's vision of the lotus in *Four Quartets*.

But such harmony in nature is not what Taoists mean by the 'elements'. The five elements formed by the interaction of Yang and Yin from the primordial substance are found in all physical manifestations; these are water, fire, wood, metal and earth. Taoists believe human nature itself to be directed by powerful forces, and an individual's date of birth encompasses particular element qualities. We shall find that wood is in many ways equivalent to the Western air element, since it is chiefly concerned with the thinking processes. In Chinese (Ch'an or Zen) Buddhism, the wooden horse is the frozen mind and the wooden man has a frozen mind. Metal, in its qualities of resolution and radical change, in many ways reflects the Eastern view of Western man: an equivalent perhaps to our opinion of the less direct oriental manner as 'inscrutable'.

For a fuller discussion on the Chinese view of the elements see *T'ung Shu, The Ancient Chinese Almanac*, edited by Martin Palmer.

Appendix C Sensitive, Sensation, Physical and Intuition: Some Definitions

The following definitions from the *Shorter Oxford Dictionary* may be helpful.

Sensation
Earth 'A particular impression received by one of the organs of sense.' (Tasting, seeing, hearing, smelling, feeling)
Water 'A mental feeling,' i.e., intuitive feeling. 'An emotion.'
Fire 'Mental apprehension, sense, or realization of something.'

Sensitive
Earth 'Having the function of sensuous perception, connected with the senses.'
Water 'With ref. to mental feelings, impressionable.'
Water or fire (As a noun) 'One sensitive to spiritualist or other occult influences.'

N.B: Air, being the reasoning process, has no part in sensation, sensitivity or intuition. People who function strongly in air may not experience any of the above vividly or consciously. The air process, however, sifted and arranged these definitions.

Physical
All four elements are physical when we experience them in the outside world, using them to support existence.
Fire, water, earth and air 'Pertaining to material nature. Belonging to the science of physics.' But earth is the only physical/psychological element and indicates functioning through the bodily or animal senses. 'Of the body; bodily, corporeal.'

Intuition

The immediate knowledge ascribed to angelic and spiritual beings with whom vision and knowledge are identical (scholastic definition of 1652).

Modern philosophy

1. The immediate apprehension of an object by the mind without the intervention of any reasoning process.
2. Immediate apprehension by the intellect alone. (This is the fiery 'leap' from a set of facts, described by Jacobi as Jung's 'intuitive speculative thinking'. It is *not* a thinking, reasoning process.)
3. Immediate apprehension by sense. (This is earth-intuition.)
4. Direct or immediate insight. (This is Jung's innervating intuition.)
5. J.B. Priestly: 'What we *feel* and what we *do*, we may be said to know by intuition.' (This *Oxford Dictionary* note describes feeling intuition – 'gut reaction'.)

Chapter Notes

Introduction

1. *The Descent of Man*.
2. The ancient religions and philosophies which include the four elements vary within their own sects, and do not embody a blanket approach to any one symbol or ritual. Tantric Buddhism, for example, is strongly linked to Gnosticism; the word *tantra* means thread, and is thought to indicate teachings which were passed on verbally through lengthy initiation because they were too secret to be written down. Sacred fire is burned at the altar in Roman Catholic and Anglican churches, but not amongst the more evangelical sects. It is impossible to make all these distinctions in a short, impressionistic view, and further readings on sectarian texts is advisable. The Authorized version (1538) of the Bible is quoted throughout.
3. Helen Gardner in *The Composition of 'Four Quartets'* (Faber and Faber, 1978), p. 21, quotes Eliot's remarks on the composition of 'Little Gidding' which, he said, would complete the relationship of the poem to the four elements by adding fire.
4. 'Our capacity for deceiving ourselves about the operation of our brain is almost limitless, mainly because we can only report a fraction of what goes on in our head. This is why much of philosophy has been barren for more than 2000 years and is likely to remain so until philosophers learn to understand the language of information processing.' F.H.C. Crick, *Scientific American*.
5. See Appendix A for the basis of this claim.

Chapter 1   Fire

1. The Rig Veda, the oldest sacred book of Hindu scriptures, is thought by Basham to have been virtually complete by 900 BC. Its ideas were brought to the Indus valley by the Arya who spoke a language of mixed European derivation.
2. Judges 13: 20
3. Exodus 3: 2.
4. *Herodian*, Book 1.

5. In *Early Middle English Texts*, B. Dickens and R.M. Wilson (eds), Bowes and Bowes 1959.
6. Information on Kempo Buddhist teachings can be obtained from the Cheirological Society (founded 1889), 29 London Road, Dereham, Norfolk. SAE please.
7. Classical descriptions of Druidism throughout Gaul and Britain are the most contemporary and convincing. See *Caesar*, p. 114–15; also Pliny and Lucan.
8. The Victoria *History of Herefordshire*, Vol. 1, 1908–78, Hereford County Library.
9. From *The Fall of the Angels* (author's translation), Sweet's *Anglo-Saxon Reader*.
10. See Appendix B.
11. *Psychology and the East, Jung*.
12. I Corinthians 7: 9.
13. See Appendix C
14. Jung, op. cit.

Chapter 2   Water
1. *Richard II*, III. iii. 54.
2. The origins of the 'Davy Jones' Locker'; referred to by sailors, are too obscure for speculation.
3. Grendel and his mother figure in the Legend of Beowulf, known throughout North-West Europe. See Whitelock.
4. Marjorie Rowling records her maid's warning in *Folklore of the Lake District*, 1976. See Westwood.
5. Letter from Pope Gregory to Abbot Mellitus on his departure for Britain in AD 601. Bede's *Ecclesiastical History*, Book 1, chapter 30, available in the British Library.
6. *Holy Wells*, R.C. Hope, 1893. Quoted by Anderson.
7. Exodus 14: 21–29.
8. Exodus 9: 22; 7: 19.
9. Genesis 6: 5–22.
10. *Lunaception*, Louise Lacey, Warner Books, New York. Quoted with other water/moon phenomena in Watson.
11. Genesis 24: 45.
12. John 4: 5–15.
13. *Timaeus*, p. 99, Plato.
14. *Thraliana*, K.C. Balderstone. Quoted in *The Pelican Guide to English Literature*, Vol. 5, 1967.
15. *Hymns of the Kingdom*, no. 92, H. Montague Butler (1833–1918).
16. 'Positivism' was the name given to the French secular religion of science. See Cobban.

Chapter 3   Air
1. *Herodian*, Book IV.
2. *A History of the Nations*, Hutchinson, c. 1914.

3. Especially Plato and the Neo-platonists of the first two or three centuries after Christ. See pp. 92–3.
4. 1 Thessalonians 4: 17.

Chapter 4   Earth

1. Exodus 20: 25. Deuteronomy 27: 5–6.
2. See Hadingham and Gooch.
3. *Folklore of the Welsh Border*, Jacqueline Simpson, Batsford, 1976. Quoted by Bord.
4. Annual Report of the Bureau of American Ethnology, Washington, 1966. Quoted by Bord.
5. See *World's Religions*.
6. *Herodian*, Book 1.
7. 'Symbols of Life', Celia Gardner, *The Countryman*, Vol 65, no. 2, 1965. Quoted by Bord.
8. See Hall whose book was originally published in 1928 as *An Encylopaedic Outline of Masonic, Hermetic, Qabalistic and Rosicrucian Symbolical Philosophy*.
9. John Piper's 1966 tapestry in Winchester Cathedral depicts the four elements with the symbols of the four evangelists and reconciles them with the Trinity.
10. Ezekiel 1: 4, 5, 10.
11. Described by Levi as 'occult agreement', the Qabalah (Kabbalah, Cabala) evolved in Southern France and Spain during the thirteenth century. Its esoteric philosophy centred on the symbolic meaning of biblical texts and claimed to revive the old mystical teachings of Moses and earlier sages. It is not acknowledged by orthodox Judaism.
12. Revelations 4: 6–8.
13. See Bierewaltes and Cox.
14. See Hixson.
15. See Lau.
16. *Julius Caesar*, 111. ii. 254.
17. Shakespeare's Sonnet CXLVI.
18. Romans 8:1–8 See also Paul's dream in Acts 10: 15.
19. I Corinthians 7: 9.
20. *The Witch-Cult in Western Europe* (Chronicles of Lanercost), OUP, 1921.
21. *The Travels of St Samson of Dol*, E.G. Bowen, Aberystwyth Studies XIII, 1934. Quoted by Anderson.
22. Eliade's comment.
23. *The Notebook of Samuel Butler*, Jonathan Cape, 1913.
24. *Kangaroo* (1923). Lawrence's 'great religion, my belief in the blood', intensifies in the later works of 1923–8.

Chapter 5   The Elements Within

1. British Library manuscript.
2. See Copleston. See note 6 below on Hermetic knowledge.
3. Quoted in Inglis. Gaub quotes Galen's 'Quod animi mores corporis temperamenta sequantur.'
4. *Henry V*, II. i. 58.

5. Paracelsus was born Theophrastus Bombastus von Hohenheim.
6. The Hermetic Corpus included the lore of Thoth and Hermes, the Egyptian and Greek gods of wisdom. Its texts are still sought after by those who believe it holds the secrets of creation and rebirth.
7. The signs of the zodiac are divided into element triplicities:

Fire	*Water*	*Earth*	*Air*
Aries	Cancer	Capricorn	Libra
Leo	Scorpio	Taurus	Aquarius
Sagittarius	Pisces	Virgo	Gemini

Fire and air are considered positive, water and earth negative.
8. Fifteenth-century manuscript, available in the British Library.
9. Astrology was never specifically banned in statutes against witchcraft or heresy. *An Astrological Discourse* (**R.** Harvey, 1583) asserted that there was no law against astrology as such, but practitioners were aware of their sensitive position. See Thomas, p. 347 and Robbins.
10. There was nothing in the vernacular between the Anglo-Saxon Gospels and John Wycliffe's Middle English translation.
11. *A Short Textbook of Medicine,* Houston, Joiner and Trounce, English Universities Press, 1962.
12. See Steinbach and Scheimann.
13. From *Philosophia Occulta,* translated by Frary Hartmann. Quoted by Hall.
14. In his commentary on the *De Anima* of Aristotle. See Copleston.
15. Mim Topliss Green, who has made a private study of the four elements in cheirology.
16. *Sun Signs,* Linda Goodman.
17. The broad, tool-using hand has changed little in two million years. Man ceased to walk on all fours in order that his hands might be free for constructive uses. The adaptation of his hands from being primarily suited to swinging from tree branches, to having the ability to handle tools, occurred from five to two million years ago.
18. See note 3, chapter 8.
19. *The Diaries of Samuel Pepys,,* pp. 81 and 270. Geddes asserts that 'Sidrophel' was Lilly.
20. See Altick.
21. See Murray Jones.
22. Inglis.

Chapter 6   In Our Element

1. *Analytical Psychology.*
2. See Whyte, Inglis, Gregory, Pearce, Freud.
3. *Psychology and the East.*
4. *The Psychology of the Unconscious,* Vol. 5, 1917. Found in The Collected Works, entitled *Symbols of Transformation.*
5. *Man and his Symbols.*
6. *Psychological Types,* Vol. 6, 1921. Found in The Collected Works.
7. *Analytical Psychology.*
8. Ibid.
9. Ibid.

10. In his final work, *Man and His Symbols*.
11. *Psychological Types*.
12. Ibid.
13. See Jacobi, an excellent introduction to Jung. See also Fordham.
14. In *Relating*.
15. *Analytical Psychology*.
16. *Man and His Symbols*.
17. *Psychology and the East*.
18. *Analytical Psychology*.
19. See Rose.
20. See Lu Ku'an Yu.
21. *What Your Handwriting Reveals*, Gullan-Whur. The four Jungian functions in handwriting are discussed in *The Graphology Workbook*.
22. *Essay on Man*, Pope.

Chapter 7   The Other Elements
1. *Psychological Types*, Jung. Found in The Collected Works.
2. Pagels.
3. See Arroyo.
4. Jung, op. cit.
5. See Teillard.
6. Jung, op. cit.
7. Ibid.
8. Ibid.
9. Arroyo uses these classical terms to avoid 'masculine' and 'feminine' which can be misunderstood.
10. *Henry V*, III. vi. 22.
11. W. de Haereyd Graig Anelog. His booklet on *Natural Psychology* can be obtained from 10 Lady Somerset Road, London NW5 1UP. £1.75 including postage and packing.
12. The three scientists of *Not in Our Genes* (Rose) assess the 'philosophical minefield which surrounds the concept of truth and which we will avoid by offering an essentially operational definition that is appropriate for assessing statements of truth in science, at least. In this definition, a true statement about an event, phenomenon, or process in the real material world must be (a) capable of independent verification by different observers; (b) internally self-consistent; (c) consistent with other statements about related events, phenomena, or process; and (d) capable of generating verifiable predictions, or hypotheses, about what will happen to the event, phenomenon, or process if it is operated upon in certain ways – if we act upon it'.
13. The possibility of implanting an embryo in the bowel wall of a male body (*The Times*, 9.5.86) could only occur to the air-fire rocket!

Chapter 8   Towards a Balance
1. *The Expression of the Emotions in Man and Animals*.
2. See Rose.
3. See Pearce. Note the work of those connected with the Bristol Cancer

Help Centre, Grove House, Cornwallis Grove, Clifton, Bristol BS8 4PG.
 4. See Gauquelin. In addition, the Astrological Association publishes its own journal of research – *Correlation*. For all information on astrology contact The Astrological Association, BM Astrology, London WC1 3XX. SAE please.
 5. *Hamlet*, IV. vii. 180.
 6. The belief of Campbell and other anthropologists. The Commonwealth Institute Exhibition of 1985–6, on man's relationship with the environment, was designed to draw public attention to this point.
 7. *Psychology and the East*.
 8. Heraclitus. Quoted by Huxley.
 9. See Wilson.
10. See Arroyo and Young.
11. Plato's *Timaeus*.
12. Ibid.
13. See Lu Ku'an Yu.
14. See Wilson.

Appendix A   Brain and Mind
 1. See Asimov.
 2. See Sagan.
 3. See Koestler.
 4. See Rose.
 5. See Gilling and Brightwell.
 6. *Scientific American*.
 7. *Two Essays on Analytical Psychology*, Vol. 7, 1953. Found in The Collected Works.

Selective Bibliography

Adler, Alfred, *What Life Should Mean to You*, Allen and Unwin, 1980.
Altick, Richard D., *Victorian People and Ideas*, Dent, 1973.
Anglo-Saxon Chronicles, The, G.R. Garmonsway (trans.), Everyman's Library, Dent/Dutton, 1953.
Anderson, M.D., History and Imagery in British Churches, John Murray, 1971.
Archer, N.P., *The Sufi Mystery*, Octagon Press, 1961.
Arroyo, Stephen, *Astrology, Psychology and the Four Elements*, CPRS Books (USA), 1975.
Asimov, I., *Guide to Science Part 2*, The Biological Sciences, Pelican Books, 1975.
Barash, David, *The Whisperings Within*, Fontana, 1981.
Barber, Richard; Riches, Anne, *A Dictionary of Fabulous Beasts*, Macmillan, 1971.
Basham, A.L. 'Hinduism', see Zaehner.
Bede, *A History of the English Church and People*, L. Sherley-Price, (trans.) Penguin Classics, 1970.
Beresford Ellis, Peter, *Celtic Inheritance*, Muller, 1985.
Bierewaltes, W., *Neoplatonism and Early Christian Thought*, Variorum Publications, 1981.
Blake, William, *For the Sexes:* The Gates of Paradise., c. 1790.
Blofeld, John, *I-Ching: The Book of Change*, Allen and Unwin, 1984.
Bord, Janet and Colin, *Earth Rites*, Paladin/Granada, 1982.
Branston, Barry, *The Lost Gods of England*, Thames and Hudson, 1974.
Bryant, Arthur, *The Age of Chivalry*, Collins, 1963.
Bryant, Christopher, *Jung and the Christian Way*, Darton, Longman and Todd, 1983.
Bunyan, John, *A Pilgrim's Progress* (1678), Lutterworth Press, 1947.
Burton, Robert (Democritus Junior), *The Anatomy of Melancholy*, 1628, available in the British Library.
Caesar, Julius, *Commentaries on His Wars in Gaul*, 1737, available in the British Library.
Campbell, Bernard, *Human Ecology*, Heinemann Educational Books, 1983.
Capra, Fritjof, *The Tao of Physics*, Wildwood House, 1982; Fontana, 1983.

de Chardin, Teilhard, *The Heart of Matter*, René Hague (trans.), Collins, 1978. See also *The Phenomenon of Man* and *The Divine Milieu*, Collins.

Chaucer, Geoffrey, *The Complete Works* (c. 1390), F.N. Robinson (ed.) OUP, 1966.

Clark, George, *Early Modern Europe*, OUP Paperback, 1966.

Clark, Grahame, *World Prehistory: An Outline*, OUP, 1977.

Cobban, Alfred, *A History of Modern France*, Pelican, 1961.

Cooper, J.C., *Symbolism*, Aquarian Press, 1982.

Cooper, J.C., *Yin and Yang*, Aquarian Press, 1981.

Copleston, Frederick, *Thomas Aquinas*, Search Press, 1955.

Cosmographiae Introductio, With Its Geogmetical and Astronomical Principles (1524), British Library.

Cox, Michael, *Mysticism*, Aquarian Press, 1983.

Craig, Hardin, *English Religious Drama of the Middle Ages*, OUP, 1955.

Da Liu, *The Tao and Chinese Culture*, Routledge and Kegan Paul, 1981.

Darwin, Charles, *The Origin of Species*, Penguin, 1949.
        The Descent of Man, John Murray, 1871.
        The Expression of the Emotions in Man and Animals, Watts & Co., 1873.

Davie, C.H., *The History of the Inquisition*, Ward & Co., 1950.

Descartes, René, *Discourse de la Méthode* with *Meditations of the First Philosophy* and *Principles of Philosophy*, Everyman's Library, Dent/Dutton, 1977.
        Philosophical Writings, Anscombe and Geach (eds.), Nelson's University Paperbacks, 1954.

Dobyns, Zipporah, *Finding the Person in the Horoscope*, Kosmos, USA.

Eliade, Mircea, *Patterns in Comparative Religion*, Allen and Unwin, 1958.
        Myth and Reality, Allen and Unwin, 1964.

Eliot, T.S., *The Collected Poems* 1909–1962, Faber and Faber, 1974.

Engels, Frederick, *Dialectics of Nature*, Progress Publishers, Moscow, 1934.

Essenes, The Gospels of The (The Communions), Edmond Bordeaux Szekely (trans. & ed.), C.W. Daniel Co., 1976.

Farquhar, George, *The Beaux-Stratagem*, Everyman's Library, Dent/Dutton, 1912.

Fenimore Cooper, J., *The Last of the Mohicans*, (1826), Collins, 1953.

Fidler, J. Havelock, *Ley Lines. Their Nature and Properties*, Turnstone, 1983.

Fordham, Frieda, *An Introduction to Jung's Psychology*, Pelican, 1953.

Frazer, James, *The Golden Bough* (1890), Macmillan, 1935.

Freud, S., *Introductory Lectures on Psychoanalysis* (1915–16), 2 Vols., Pelican Books 1973.

Gaub, Jerome, *De Regimine Mentis;* in Rather, L.J., *Mind and Body in the Eighteenth Century*, Wellcome Historical Medical Library, 1965.

Gauquelin, Michel, *The Truth about Astrology*, Hutchinson Paperbacks, 1984.

Geddes, Sheila, *The Art of Astrology*, Aquarian Press, 1980.

Gellner, Ernest, *The Psychoanalytic Movement*, Paladin/Granada, 1985.

Gettings, Fred, *The Book of the Hand*, Hamlyn Books, 1965.

Gibran, Kahlil, *The Prophet* (1926), Heinemann, 1926.

Gilling, Dick; Brightwell, Robin, *The Human Brain*, Orbis Publishing, 1982.

Gooch, Stan, *Guardians of the Ancient Wisdom*, Wildwood House, 1979.

Graves, Tom, *Needles of Stone*, Turnstone, 1980.

Green, Liz, *Relating*, Coventure, 1977.

Gregory, Marcus, *Psychotherapy, Scientific and Religious*, Macmillan, 1939.

Gullan-Whur, Margaret, *What Your Handwriting Reveals*, Aquarian Press, 1984.
      The Graphology Workbook, Aquarian Press, 1986.

Hadingham, Evan, *Circles and Standing Stones*, Heinemann, 1975.

Hall, Manly P., *The Secret Teachings of All Ages*, Aquarian Press, 1983.

Hardy, Alister, *The Biology of God*, Jonathan Cape, 1975.

Hartleib, Johann, *Die Kunst Chiromantia* (1448); in Allen, E.H. (trans.), *A Manual of Cheirosophy, Cheirognomy and Cheiromancy*, 1885, available in the British Library.

Herodian, C.R. Whittaker (trans.), 4 Vols, Heinemann, 1969.

Hixon, Joseph, *The Human Body*, Cooper Square Publications, USA, 1966.

Humble, Richard, *The Saxon Kings*, Weidenfeld and Nicholson, 1980.

Humphreys, Christmas. *Buddhism*, Pelican, 1951.

Huxley, Francis, *The Way of the Sacred*, Aldus/Jupiter Books, 1974.

Inglis, Brian, *A History of Medicine*, Weidenfeld and Nicholson, 1965.

Jackson and Allen, *Astrology in the Renaissance*, Routledge and Kegan Paul, 1983.

Jacobi, Jolande, *The Psychology of C.G. Jung*, Routledge and Kegan Paul, 1969.

Jung, C.G. *The Collected Works*, Routledge and Kegan Paul, 1953.
      Analytical Psychology (The Tavistock Lectures 1934), Routledge and Kegan Paul, 1968.
      Psychology and the East, Routledge and Kegan Paul, 1978.

Jung, C.G. and others, *Man and his Symbols*, Aldus/Jupiter Books, 1964.

Kenton, Warren, *Astrology*, Avon Books, USA, 1974.

Kirby, D.P., *The Making of Early England*, Batsford, 1967.

Kitson, Peter, *The Age of Baroque*, Landmarks of the World's Art, Hamlyn, 1966.

Knapton, E.J., *Europe 1450–1815*, John Murray, 1958.

Koestler, Arthur, *The Ghost in the Machine*, Hutchinson, 1957.

Koyré, Alexander, Introduction to *Philosophical Writings*, see Descartes.

Lamb, Charles, *Essays of Elia*, Blackie & Son, 1823.

Lau, Theodora, *Chinese Horoscopes*, Arrow Books, 1979.

Leach, Maria (ed.), *A Dictionary of Folklore, Mythology and Legend*, New English Library, 1972.

Lévi, Eliphas, *The Mysteries of the Qabalah*, Aquarian Press, 1981.

Lewis, C.S., *The Four Loves*, Collins Fount Paperbacks, 1960.

Llewellyn, George, *A–Z Horoscope Maker and Delineator. A Textbook of Astrology*, Llewellyn Publications, USA, 1972.

Lommel, Andreas, *Prehistoric and Primitive Man*, Landmarks of the World's Art, Hamlyn, 1966.

Longfellow, Henry Wadsworth, *The Song of Hiawatha*, Dent, 1960.

Lovelock, James, *The Gaia Hypothesis*, Routledge and Kegan Paul, 1984.

Lu Ku'an Yu, *Ch'an and Zen Teaching*, Rider and Co., 1961.

Lurker, Manfred, *The Gods and Symbols of Ancient Egypt*, Thames and Hudson, 1980.

Mackenzie, Donald A., *Ancient Man in Britain*, Blackie & Sons, 1922.

Maslow, Abraham, *Motivation and Personality*, Harper & Bros., 1954.

Maslow, Abraham (with Mittelmann), *Principles of Abnormal Psychology*, Harper & Bros., 1941.

Mayr, Ernst, *Animal Species and Evolution*, Belknap Press (Harvard), 1963.

Michell, John. *The View over Atlantis*, Abacus Books, 1973.

Milman, H.H., *A History of Christianity*, Vol. 3., John Murray, 1863.

du Moulin, Antoine, *Vraye et Parfaicte Chiromancie et Phisionomie*, 1620, British Library.

Murray Jones, Peter, *Medieval Medical Miniatures*, British Library Publication, 1985.

McIntosh, Christopher, *The Rosy Cross Unveiled*, Aquarian Press, 1980.

Oates, Joan, *Babylon*, Thames and Hudson, 1979.

Oedipus Aegyptiacus, Kirchner, A., available in the British Library.

Owst, G.R., *Preaching in Medieval England*, CUP, 1926.

Oxford Dictionary (*Shorter*), 3rd edn, 1970.

Pagels, Elaine, *The Gnostic Gospels*, Weidenfeld and Nicholson, 1980.

Palmer, Martin (ed.), *T'ung Shu, The Ancient Chinese Almanac*, Rider & Co., 1986.

Pearce, Ian, *The Gate of Healing*, Neville Spearman, 1983.

Pegg, Bob, *Rites and Riots. Folk Customs of Britain and Europe*, Blandford, 1981.

Pepys, Samuel, *The Diaries of Samuel Pepys*, Everyman's Library, Dent/Dutton, 1953.

Picard, Barbara Leonie, *Tales of the Norse Gods and Heroes*, OUP, 1972.

Plato, *Timaeus and Critias*, Desmond Lee (trans.), Penguin Classics, 1965.

Pope, Alexander, *The Collected Poems*, OUP Paperbacks, 1978.

Potter, Simeon, *Our Language*, Pelican, 1950.

Ragozin, Zenaide A., *Vedic India*, Munshi Ram Manohar Lal, Delhi, 1961.

Robbins, Rossell Hope, *Encyclopaedia of Witchcraft and Demonology*, Crown, New York, 1972.

Rose, Kamin and Lewonton, *Not in Our Genes:* Biology, Ideology and Human Nature, Pantheon and Penguin Books, 1984.

Rutherford, Ward, *The Druids: Magicians of the West*, Aquarian Press, 1978.

Sagan, Carl, *The Dragons of Eden*, Hodder and Stoughton, 1979.

Scheimann, Eugene, *A Doctor's Guide to Better Health through Palmistry*, Parker, New York, 1969.

Scientific American, *The Brain*, W.H. Freeman & Co., 1979.

Singh, Maharaj Charan; see Arroyo.

Spencer, Herbert, *First Principles*, 1862, British Library.
                    The Principles of Psychology, 1855, British Library.

Spenser, Edmund, *The Fairie Queene*, in Poets of the English Language, Eyre and Spottiswoode and Heron Books.

Stapleton, Michael, *A Dictionary of Greek and Roman Mythology*, Hamlyn, 1978.

Starzecka, Dorota, *Hawaii: People and Culture*, British Museum Publications, 1975.

Steinbach, Martin, *Medical Palmistry*, New Jersey University Books, 1975.

Storr, Anthony, *The Art of Psychotherapy*, Secker and Warburg/Heinemann, 1979.

Strong, Donald E., *The Classical World*, Landmarks of the World's Art, Hamlyn, 1965.

Suttie, Ian D., *The Origins of Love and Hate* (1935). Routledge and Kegan Paul, 1960.

Sweet, *Anglo-Saxon Reader* (revised by Dorothy Whitelock), OUP, 1970.

Tagore, Rabindranath, *Collected Poems and Plays*, Macmillan, 1936.

Teillard, Ania, *L'Ame et L'Ecriture*, Editions Traditionelles, Paris, 1983.

Thomas, Keith, *Religion and the Decline of Magic*, Weidenfeld and Nicholson, 1971.

Thompson, J. Eric S., *Maya Hieroglyphs without Tears,* British Museum Publications, 1972.

Tripp, Edward, *Crowell's Handbook of Classical Mythology*, New York, 1980.

Victoria, History of Herefordshire, 1908–78, Hereford County Library.

Waechter, John, *Man before History*, Phaidon Press, 1976.

Walker, Benjamin, *Gnosticism*, Aquarian Press, 1983.

Watkins, Alfred, *The Ley Hunter's Manual*, Turnstone, 1983.

Watson, Lyall, *Supernature*, Coronet Books, 1983.

Westwood, Jennifer, *Albion: A Guide to Legendary Britain*, Granada, 1985.

Whitlock, Ralph, *In Search of Lost Gods*, Phaidon Press, 1979.

Whyte, L.L., *The Unconscious before Freud*, Julian Friedmann, 1978.

Wilcock, John, *A Guide to Occult Britain*, Sidgwick and Jackson, 1976.

Williams, J., *Druidopaedia: The Druidical System of Education*, 1823, Hereford County Library.

Wilson, Colin, *Lord of the Underworld:* Jung and the Twentieth Century, Aquarian Press, 1984.

    The War against Sleep: The Philosophy of Gurdjieff, Aquarian Press, 1980.

Wilson, E.O., *Sociobiology: The New Synthesis,* Harvard University Press, 1975.

World's Religions, The, Lion Books, 1982.

Young, Arthur, *The Geometry of Meaning*, Robert Briggs Associates, 1976.

Zaehner, R.H. (ed.), *The Encyclopaedia of Living Faiths*, Hutchinson, 1959.

Zwalf, W., *Heritage of Tibet*, British Museum Publications, 1981.

Index